Becoming His Princess:
A Study Based on the Life of Sarah

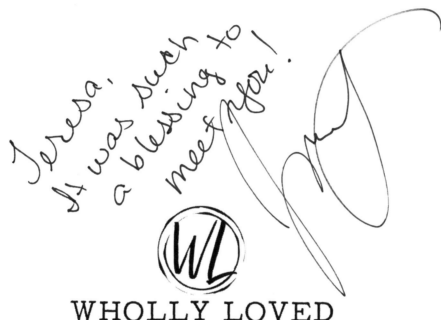

WHOLLY LOVED

Written by Jennifer Slattery
With Contributions from Susan Aken, Jessica Brodie, Cheri Cowell, and Dena Dyer

Becoming His Princess: A Study Based on the Life of Sarah

Wholly Loved Ministries, Omaha, NE.

Helping women find spiritual and emotional freedom as they learn to live wholly and deeply loved by God.

For more information, visit WhollyLoved.com

All Scripture quotations are taken from:

The *Holy Bible, New International Version*, Copyright © 1973, 1978, 1984 by the International Bible Society. THE HOLY BIBLE, NEW INTERNATIONAL VERSION®, NIV® Copyright © 1973, 1978, 1984, 2011 by Biblica, Inc.® Used by permission. All rights reserved worldwide.

The ESV® Bible (The Holy Bible, English Standard Version), copyright © 2001 by Crossway, a publishing ministry of Good News Publishers. All rights reserved.

© 2018 by Wholly Loved Ministries

All rights reserved. No part of this book may be reproduced, transmitted, or stored in any type of retrieval system without permission in writing from Wholly Loved Ministries.

ISBN: 9781729587515

Cover design by Jennifer Slattery and Ashley Slattery

Brought to you by the creative team at Wholly Loved Ministries: Senior Editor and Editor of Biblical Accuracy, Yvonne Anderson; Copyeditor, LaShawn Montoya; Production and Design, Jennifer Slattery.

Published in the United States of America.

Table of Contents:

Week One: Reclaiming Our Identity ………………………………………………………….. P. 1

Week Two: An Unshakable Security ……………………………………….……..……..….. p. 23

Week Three: Remaining Faithful Through Discouragements ………………………………….p. 39

Week Four: Fear, Faith, & the God Who Saves …………………………………………….. p. 59

Week Five: Waiting Well ………………………………………………………....………… p. 81

Week Six: Moving Past Self-Sufficiency ……………………..…………………..………....p. 99

Week Seven: Living in Grace ……………………………………………………..……….. p. 119

Introduction:
By Jennifer Slattery

Useless. Unwanted. Bad. The person who, somehow, sabotaged everything good.

I don't know how or when those labels first formed, but over time, they sank deeper into my heart, until, by my sophomore year, I became the person I believed I was—the problem teen. The bothersome kid people tolerated in spurts but no one really wanted around.

I was *that* type of girl, the one who bounced from party to party, boyfriend to boyfriend, numbing my pain and feelings of worthlessness with massive quantities of alcohol until I landed on the streets of Tacoma, Washington.

But in the middle of my despair and hopelessness, God reached down and pulled me out. Through grace, He transformed this former homeless, high school dropout bent on self-destruction to a passionate, life-breathing and life-giving woman of God. This transformation came slowly, so slowly, there were periods when I felt stagnant, stuck between who I once was and who God was calling me to be.

I knew intellectually that I was a redeemed child of God, but my wounded heart refused to own those truths. I could explain God's grace to others, but I couldn't fathom how Christ could love me. It seemed no amount of truth, of Scripture memorization, or Bible studies could dislodge all those lies wedged in my heart.

Those lies impacted everything—my behavior, reactions, relationships, and perceptions of myself, others, and situations. They plunged me into isolation, into hiding, and kept me from living as Christ's radiant treasure.

But then God stripped away everything false and insufficient so I could find secure footing in Him alone.

Sarah's Journey

He brought Sarah, a devalued, displaced, and infertile woman from ancient Mesopotamia, on a similar journey. Living in a time when women were auctioned as brides to the highest bidder, valued for what they could do, or rather, produce over who they were, Sarah must've viewed herself as a commodity.

A possession with one purpose—to have children.

Can you imagine the pain, the shame and sense of worthlessness, she experienced when she couldn't fulfill the primary reason, supposedly, she'd been placed on earth for?

For decades, she lived as the woman who never measured up, but who learned, in a miraculous way, that she didn't need to. She didn't need to prove herself or fulfill certain societal norms. She simply needed to believe—to realize and accept—that God loved her, had a plan for her, and was working out that plan.

She needed to find her worth in Him.

God encourages us to do the same. Through this seven-week study, we invite you on a journey of becoming. As we follow Sarah's travels from Ur to the promised land, from barrenness to motherhood, and from living in shame to resting in grace, I pray God will take you on a similar adventure. Let Him purify your heart and mind of every lie and misconception until only the truth remains.

Here's the truth: You are God's princess, His masterpiece and treasure, His chosen one.

Study Overview

Here's what to expect:

- Video introduction: Short testimonial video introducing each week's topic.

- Group discussion: Questions designed to help you explore the week's theme and consider how it might apply to you.

- Daily lessons: Lessons begin with a suggested reading followed by a testimonial introduction intended to get you thinking about the day's focus. Questions pulled from that day's Bible reading follow.

Two Bible Study Application Options

The first two lessons of every week will present a Bible study application tool to help you grow in your Bible reading skills. For the first day of every week, you will have two options for this. The first option provides general questions, which will be the same each week, to help you understand the "macro-view" of the Bible. You'll consider how that week's passage relates to God's overall story of redemption, His nature, and how mankind is to relate to Him.

The second option encourages more of a "micro-view" reading and looks at things like how the passage relates to Genesis's unique theme and how to read Scripture in relation to context, syntax, and other literary elements. You may choose one option for all seven weeks or may move back and forth between the two.

Our primary goal with all Day One and Two lessons is to gain skills we can apply whenever we read Scripture. We hope the guidelines presented here can act as reference guides for years to come.

This study follows Sarah's journey, revealed in Genesis 11:27-23:20 and incorporates additional verses and passages that expand on truths presented through our primary text.

Before each group discussion, I encourage you to watch the correlating *Becoming His Princess* videos, located on our Youtube Channel (Go to YouTube and search Wholly Loved), or listen to the audio, located on SoundCloud at soundcloud.com/wholly_loved. The questions provided in each session opening will help guide your discussion.

You may find it helpful to purchase a journal to jot down your notes, thoughts, questions, applications, and prayers.

But ultimately, this is your study, so adapt it accordingly. You may not have time for much personal investigation. Or you may choose to divide each day into two or three to allow for deeper contemplation. God's desire isn't that we accumulate a lot of head knowledge or check off assignments but instead that we spend time with Him, come to know Him better, and experience life change.

He wants us to become a little more like Jesus, more like the women He created us to be. The women He knows we *can* be.

Pre-Study Homework

Before you officially begin, I encourage you to read Sarah's story in Genesis 11:27 to 23:20. The narrative begins when she left Ur and takes us to when God brought her to the ultimate Promised Land—heaven.

If possible, take a day by yourself to go somewhere quiet and read her journey in one sitting. This will help you see the big picture of Sarah's story and will provide an important backdrop for everything we'll discuss in the following weeks. Make this a special time: play soft music, visit a park, or perhaps find a quiet coffee house with comfy chairs. Consider it a date-day with Jesus and carve out space and open your heart to meet with Him. Before you begin reading, pause to ask Him to reveal Himself and His heart for you through the pages of Scripture.

If you'd rather divide the narrative into smaller portions, you can follow one of the reading guides listed on the following pages.

Reading Plan

To complete in one week:

Day 1: Gen. 11:27-32, 12:1-20, 13:1-18

Day 2: Gen. 14:1-24, 15:1-21

Day 3: Gen. 16:1-16, Gen. 17:1-27

Day 4: Gen. 18:1-33

Day 5: Gen. 19:1-38

Day 6: Gen. 20:1-18, Gen. 21:1-34

Day 7: Gen. 22:1-24, Gen. 23:1-20

To complete in two weeks:

Day 1: Gen. 11:27-32, 12:1-20

Day 2: Gen. 13:1-18

Day 3: Gen. 14:1-24

Day 4: Gen. 15:1-21

Day 5: Gen. 16:1-16

Day 6: Gen. 17:1-14

Day 7: Gen. 17:15-27

Day 8: Gen. 18:1-15

Day 9: Gen. 18:16-33

Day 10: Gen. 19:1-29

Day 11: Gen. 20:1-18

Day 12: Gen. 21:1-21

Day 13: Gen. 22:22-34

Day 14: Gen. 23:1-20

For we are God's handiwork, created in Christ Jesus for good works, which God prepared in advance for us to do. Ephesians 2:10

Week One: Reclaiming Our Identity

Jennifer Slattery

Week One: Reclaiming Our Identity
Viewer & Group Discussion Guide
From the Video:

The comments and insinuations that hurt the most are those that hit our _____ _____.

When we're grounded in our _____ the lies won't hurt us. They won't sink in.

_____ (Who we are and who we think we are) determines _____.

If we're centered in _____ and _____, we have nothing to prove and no reason to feel defeated or insecure.

When we're grounded in our identity in Christ, we're not _____ to our _____ or other people's _____, opinions, or _____.

When our ugly comes out, it's easy to focus on the symptoms—the behaviors we hate. But often, we're reacting from a _____, feeding lies formed during or directly following a painful experience or rejection.

Nothing we _____ or _____ will fill our need for significance and value.

We need to learn to question our _____ and become alert to the _____ we believe and tell ourselves so that we can live in the _____ of who we are.

Group Discussion Questions:
Note to leaders: You probably won't have time to get to all the questions. Please let the discussion guide you, and focus on those questions you feel most beneficial to your group members.

What resonated with you most during the video?

What are some of the names, positive and negative, others have called you?

How did the positive names make you feel, and why?

How did the negative names make you feel, and why?

How did your sense of identity (feeling secure in who you were) or insecurity play in to your response?

In what ways do you give lies regarding your worth or identity power over you?

Can you think of a time when your identity (whether a false sense of identity or recognition of who you are in Christ) impacted your behavior?

What does it mean to be a victim of one's emotions?

What does it mean to be a victim of other people's comments, opinions, and poor behavior?

How often do you slip into victim responses?

What is one thing you hope to gain from this study?

Day One (Option One)
Understanding God's Story
Read: Genesis 11

I'm a storyteller by nature, so I love viewing the Bible as an epic love story that spans across generations. It's the ultimate boy loves girl, loses girl, fights for girl, and seals her as His for all eternity story. God loves us, sees us, and pursues us. We spurn His love, push Him away, and rebel against Him, but He persists, and by grace, wins us over. In Christ, He secured our happily-ever-after.

You've probably heard at least part of the creation account. God created an amazing world free of sin, pain, and disease. He created humans to live and care for this world and have an intimate yet submissive relationship with Him. But God's beloved creation rebelled and paradise was shattered. The rest of Scripture reveals mankind's continued rebellion and sin, ways we've tried to reach God on our own terms rather than His, and our attempts to meet our needs apart from Him. On occasion, we see biblical characters displaying the opposite of this. They then become examples for us to follow.

And woven throughout all of this, revealed on every page, we see God's unchanging nature—His love, mercy, faithfulness, righteousness, justice, and sovereignty, all of which are ultimately revealed in the death and resurrection of Jesus Christ.

All of Scripture reveals the gospel in some way: Our need for it, the promise of it, the fulfillment of it, or its power. But even more than that, it reveals the heart, plans, power, and purposes of the One who loves us and desires to reveal Himself to us.

Read Genesis 11.

Who are the main characters in this passage?

What does this passage reveal about the human condition, such as:
- Mankind's rebellion against/obedience toward God?

- Mankind's attempts to fill their needs apart from Him or relying on Him for their needs?

- Mankind's attempts to reach Him on their own terms?

What does this passage reveal regarding God's nature?

What does this passage reveal about God's plans?

How might this passage reveal mankind's need for the gospel?

In what ways are you/have you been similar to one or more of the characters in this passage?

What might God want you to know through this section of Scripture?

What might He be asking you to do?

End your reading in prayer, asking God to help you apply the biblical truths discovered and live out whatever you sense Him impressing on your heart.

Day One (Option Two)
Bible Study Application Tool: Literary context
Read: Genesis 11

The Bible's makeup is unique. Composed of sixty-six books representing seven different genres, it unveils one over-arching redemptive story. Each book, from Genesis to Revelation, reveals specific truths regarding who God is and who we are in relation to Him. Therefore, when we read a narrative like Abram and Sarai's, we'll best understand the truths and events when viewed in the context of the Bible as a whole.

Can we pause here? As I mentioned in this week's video and audio segments, when it comes to Abraham (initially called Abram) and Sarah (initially called Sarai), I can get a little "brain-tongue-tied." For convenience purposes, we'll refer to the names God gave them in Genesis 17.

Understanding Biblical Narratives

It's important to note, narratives present certain details of a situation that reveal or illustrate a particular point. Human actions and reactions are not necessarily prescriptive. In fact, many historical events will reveal the opposite—how humans should not behave! But in every story, we'll catch glimpses of God's heart, character, and purposes.

The Basics

Let's begin with a look at Genesis, the book in which Sarah's story is found.

Genesis, the first book in the Bible, is a book of beginnings. It describes the origin of time, space, matter, the universe, man, sin, the Jewish nation, and God's covenantal relationship with humans. Keeping this in mind, let's look at how Abraham and Sarah's story fits within this book and Scripture's over-arching redemptive message.

Some questions to explore:

1. Who wrote Genesis?

2. When do scholars believe it was written?

3. What are its major theological themes?

4. What are its major historical themes?

Most Bibles provide answers to these questions at the beginning of each Bible book. Commentaries, easily found online, can also be helpful. Numerous Bible websites, like BibleTraining.org and

BibleStudyTools.com, provide in-depth information on each book of the Bible. To access this information simply type "Genesis theme" then the site name into your search engine.

Abraham and Sarah in Context

Abraham is considered the Father of the Jewish nation, and it's interesting how infrequently we see Sarah associated with this. I'm not hugely surprised, as Abraham lived in a patriarchal society where land, blessings, and family names were passed down from father to son.

And yet, it is precisely because of this that I find Sarah's story so intriguing, for by God's design and direct involvement, a once barren woman bore the "child of promise." In this and all the ways God miraculously showed up in her life, especially when she felt abandoned, discarded, and most likely worthless, I hope you'll see our Father's heart, not just for her but for you as well.

To begin our week, read or review Genesis 11, focusing on verses 27-32.

As you read, jot down anything that stands out to you as well as any questions you have.

Did you notice how, directly preceding Abraham and Sarah's story, Scripture tells us humans were trying to "make a name" for themselves, or as the NLT puts it, to make themselves "famous" (Gen. 11:4)? Then, with Abraham, God basically says He's going to do this for Abraham—to make his name great or famous.

What's the difference? Why was it wrong for mankind to elevate themselves when creating the tower of Babel when God Himself said He'd make Abraham famous?

The One Worthy of Glory

I believe the answer is three-fold. First, the tower built in chapter 11 stemmed from pride, selfishness, and disobedience. After the flood (Genesis 6-8), God told an ancient man named Noah and his descendants to multiply and fill the earth, or scatter. The men in verse 4 were attempting to prevent this from occurring. Plus, instead of bringing glory to God, which is humanity's entire reason for existence, they wanted to glorify themselves.

God had invited them to participate in His amazing, eternal story, but they were stuck in their own small narratives. Therefore, God reestablished His will and ways through Abraham and Sarah. John Piper states it this way:

> "When ancient man refused to align himself with the goal of God," Piper said, "God set about a very different way of achieving that same goal. Man"–referring to those involved with the tower of Babel—"chose to rely on himself and seek his own glory." Therefore, "God

chose one small man and promised to achieve His purposes through him and his descendants. He would make Abram's name great so that He, and not man, would get the glory.[1]"

Notice the numerous contrasts between the two narratives.

Whereas the tower of Babel began with mankind's disobedience, Abraham and Sarah's journey began in obedience. The men creating the tower relied on their strength and wisdom. Through all they experienced, God taught Abraham and Sarah to rely completely on Him. And in the end, God did what Abraham and Sarah could not—He made good on His word and gave them the long-promised child. Finally, selfishness underlay the creation of the tower of Babel; the people sought to bless themselves. God raised up Abraham and Sarah to become a blessing to all nations of all time (Gen. 12:3), a plan that culminated in the death and resurrection of Jesus Christ.

This leads us to an interesting dichotomy—self-obsession makes us miserable and leads to all sorts of ugly and destructive behaviors. Placing others above ourselves and surrendering to God's will, however, leads to life, joy, peace, and freedom. I've seen this again and again. Whatever I cling to begins to consume me. When I'm clinging to Christ and the life He offers, His Spirit floods the deepest, darkest recesses of my heart. When I cling to myself (will, desires, thoughts, agenda), my life and heart darken.

Aligning a Heart

We see this in Sarah's life as well. She longed for a child to escape the label of barrenness she'd carried so long. As we follow her story, we'll see this was God's desire as well. But He wouldn't give this precious gift to her, one meant for all people of all time, until she was able to carry it.

God wanted her heart surrendered to and aligned with His.

That's where life starts and how it's sustained. In Christ and Him alone we discover who we are and become all we're meant to be.

End today's study time in prayer, asking God to show you what He wants you to understand from today's Bible reading and how you can apply that to your life.

---

[1] Piper, John. "God Created Us For His Glory." Desiring God, July 27, 1980. https://www.desiringgod.org/messages/god-created-us-for-his-glory

Day Two
Investigating Historical Context
Review: Genesis 11

Scripture is a living, powerful, eternal, and personal book that reveals universal truths and principles applicable to all. God's truths and standards don't change with our constantly shifting culture. That said, though He created and preserved the Bible for all humanity, He also had an intended message for the original audience. His message to us today will never contradict His message to ancient man, and vice-versa.

The more we understand the original audience and God's words to them, the better we'll understand how to apply them. The text comes alive with layers and depths we likely would miss otherwise.

Infertility in Ancient Mesopotamia

For example, in our text, we learn almost immediately that Sarah was barren. Any woman who's experienced infertility knows the heartache this condition would have caused and the strain it would have placed on her and Abraham's marriage. But once one understands ancient man's view of women, societal expectations, and marriage and infertility laws, Sarah's story becomes painfully tragic and her desire more desperate. First, she lived during a time when women were viewed as property. Men could legally divorce their wives if they failed to bear children.

As you can see, uncovering the history and culture surrounding a passage adds depth to our understanding.

Questions to Investigate

Our goal, as we dig into God's Word, is to[2]:

1. Determine the original intended meaning. (What did the text mean when Sarah and Abraham were alive and when Moses, the writer, was writing it?)
2. How was the original audience and/or biblical characters' culture different from ours?
3. How was the original audience and/or biblical characters' culture similar to ours?
4. What is/are the basic truth principle(s) revealed through this narrative or passage? (Example: A person shouldn't deceive others.)
5. Is that principle consistent with the overall message and truths presented in Scripture?
6. How does that principle apply today, specifically, to you personally?

What might you want to know regarding the time period or location in which Sarah lived? List five things. If you have time, choose one to investigate further using an Internet search.

A Look at the Author

---

[2] List of questions and information taken from Grasping God's Word: A Hands-on Approach to Reading, Interpreting, and Applying the Bible by J. Scott Duvall & J. Daniel Hays.

Scholars believe Moses, the Hebrew whom God used to free His people from slavery and oppression, wrote the book of Genesis. As we consider his life and ministry, we notice some intriguing connections. First, most scholars believe the tower of Babel was the beginning of the world's first ziggurat—a temple dedicated to false gods. The people were creating a tower they hoped would allow the gods to descend to them.

Now, consider the land (and family background, religiously speaking) God called Abraham and Sarah out of. Idolatry permeated ancient Mesopotamia, the city of Ur included. God commanded Abraham and Sarah to leave their pagan homeland and family faith roots and embark on a journey of divine discovery. With every step, especially the most painful, they learned more about God, His requirements, and their relationship to Him.

This is exactly what the ancient Hebrews experienced when Moses led them out of Egypt, a land where people worshiped over 2,000 different gods! Everything from the sun and Nile River to cats and beetles. But through a series of plagues, God demonstrated His supremacy over powerless idols and cultural myths.

God is continually transforming our worldviews as well. With every step we take, as we compare our lives, thoughts, ideologies, and perceptions to the unchanging truth of Scripture, we come to know God better and discover our truest selves in Him.

As you end today's study, I encourage you to prayerfully ask Him to reveal Himself to you in a clearer or deeper way.

Day Three
That's Not My Name!
Review: Genesis 11:27-30
Read: Zephaniah 3:17, Psalm 139:13-14, Luke 12:6-7, Ephesians 1:3-5, 1 Peter 2:9

I've been called a "tornado," "pit bull", "darling," and numerous other things I don't care to repeat. Each name left an indentation in my heart. Some encouraged and uplifted me and helped bring out my best. Others baffled me, but all changed me in some way, for better or worse.

My faith journey has been a process of becoming—of learning to recognize all those lies I've adopted over the years, of tossing them out, and replacing them with truth.

"I'm worthless" became "I'm priceless."
"I'm incompetent" became "I'm empowered."
"I'm hopeless" became "I'm redeemed and restored."
"I'm insignificant" became "I'm called and commissioned."
"I'm rejected" became "I'm chosen."

Over the years, through Bible studies, prayer, and numerous encounters, God has been purging my brain and heart of everything that gets in His way and keeps me from living in freedom. He's been purifying my mud-filled glass of water.

Sarah's False Identity

God did the same for Sarah. When we first meet her, we learn: 1) She's Abram's wife, and 2) She's barren. Both labels would have impacted her sense of identity, but the latter would've been devastating. In her day, everyone considered infertility a curse—evidence the woman had in somehow displeased the gods.

But when others saw her as damaged and insufficient, God viewed her with love, and He spent the rest of her life proving this.

Her steps toward wholeness began with a rather terrifying pilgrimage as she traveled further and further from everything she knew.

Fears Rekindled

My route to healing had a similar beginning. Let me start by saying, I *hate* moving. Through the eight moves my husband and I have experienced, I've learned to adapt. But for years, every relocation triggered a near-panic reaction.

I'd grow angry, tense, irritable—in short, I'd behave like a mouthy toddler, and I hadn't a clue why. I assumed the emotions I'd suppressed for over a decade—with binging and purging, self-induced starvation, massive quantities of alcohol—were buried and gone.

They weren't. They simply festered beneath the surface, emerging unexpectedly through ugly behavior. But instead of prayerfully evaluating my emotions, I turned to self-reliance. I'd engage in some outward activity that brought comfort and control, like cleaning or exercise, or I'd isolate myself until I could produce a happier, more Christ-like Jennifer.

My False Identity

The life I was living was only a fragment of all God had in store for me. I wasn't living fully as He created me to be, attempting to produce, in my own strength, a whole and complete version of myself, something only Christ can do.

God rarely uses the comfortable to transform us. Instead, He allows life to turn up the pressure, agitate our water, and squeeze out all that putrid sediment weighting our hearts.

In the summer of 2006, our family handed our house keys to our realtor and headed to Bossier City, Louisiana, for a position we were 95.6% certain awaited my husband. That job, however, wouldn't begin for some thirty days, which meant we lived in limbo for a month.

Essentially, we were homeless. My husband thought this was great! He viewed it like an extended vacation. For me, it triggered memories of my teen years when, bouncing from place to place, hopelessness oppressed me like a heavy, dark blanket.

Getting to the Root

This event triggered numerous emotions. But what completely paralyzed me and churned my stomach were all the lies developed during that time. In remembering what had happened, I remembered who *I'd been*, who I believed I still was.

God knew that. He knew my tendency to cling to the lies of my past, and so, bit by bit, sermon after sermon, and song after song, He chiseled away at my false identity.

One afternoon, while we were staying in some mid-priced hotel somewhere between Nevada and Colorado, an old acquaintance sent me an email. We weren't terribly close, and though we'd served together in ministry, our conversations never went deep. She knew nothing of my past.

She knew me as the woman who taught Sunday school and made fresh squeezed lemonade, who stayed on top of laundry, and spent Saturday afternoons in her flower garden. She didn't know the drunken teen who wandered the streets of Tacoma, Washington, looking for a place a crash.

But her email was so … applicable, appropriate … as if she knew.

She didn't, but God did, and through her message telling of a pastor's son engaged to a former prostitute, He spoke directly to my broken heart.

An Image of Grace

In the account, the fiancé and his beloved belonged to a small church, and I suspect the bride-to-be had been part of their community for some time. She went to Sunday school, brought side dishes to potlucks, and engaged in small talk over purses and dresses and new fashion designs.

All the while hiding who she'd been, who she feared—believed—she still was.

She was *that* kind of woman, the type other ladies avoided and moms warned their sons to stay away from. She felt certain, eventually, everyone would come to recognize who she was and want nothing to do with her. But one day, a kind, godly young man saw something different in her, something beautiful and precious. Oh, how she wanted to believe his estimation of her! How she needed his love and acceptance! And so, when he knelt before her one day, ring in hand, she stifled her fear of rejection and exposure and said yes.

All the while, she was waiting for everyone else to recognize the worthless, sinful woman she really was and toss her aside.

Then one day, it happened. Somehow, her past got out, and the church flew into an uproar. Fueled with self-righteousness, they called a meeting. Then, once everyone had gathered—all the elders and mothers and grandmothers and children—one of them stood and disclosed, point by shameful point, her story.

No one could understand how a pastor's son, a righteous and respectable man, could ever marry someone so scandalous.

But then, her fiancé rose. Eyes locked on her, he replied, "Are you saying God's grace isn't good enough for her?"

God's Message to Me

As I read that, tears poured down my face, because I knew God was asking me that same question. "Are you saying My grace isn't good enough for you?"

Perhaps He's asking you that same question. What are you holding on to? What is keeping you from resting fully in Christ's grace? What lies have you come to believe about yourself? What false identities have you adopted?

Pause before you begin today's Bible reading to give those to God and ask Him to free you. Ask Him to show you, as He did me, and I believe, as He did Sarah, how beautiful, priceless, and loved you are.

Whatever labels outside of Christ you've been carrying, hear what God's saying to you: That is not your name!

Review Genesis 11:27-30.

How might the label of barrenness have affected Sarah's sense of self?

When have you allowed a role (or lack thereof) to define you?

How or when can good labels become harmful?

As I mentioned earlier, in Sarah's day, men could legally divorce their wives if they failed to get pregnant. Though this rarely occurred as the man would also have to return her dowry, how do you think this practice made women feel?

When have you felt dispensable?

Read the following verses and list what each tells you about God's love for you and your value to Him.

Zephaniah 3:17

Psalm 139:13-14

Luke 12:6-7

Ephesians 1:3-5

1 Peter 2:9

Choose one of the above verses to write on a notecard and prayerfully think about this week. If you really want to take steps toward freedom, memorize it. Ask God to help you view yourself as He sees you.

Day Four
Redefined by God
Review: Genesis 11:27-30
Read: 1 Timothy 1:12-17

I ended a whirlwind weekend spent running from one speaking engagement to another with one thought: *I don't want to be the homeless girl.*

I didn't want my past to define me. Though God had used my testimony in a powerful way to point numerous broken men and women to Him, I struggled to rest, fully, in His grace. To let His grace, and not my time wandering the streets of Tacoma, define me.

To me, that one name, "homeless girl," carried so many others, like "failure," "ignorance," and "ungodliness." During that time, when many of my peers began considering college and taking steps toward adulthood, I pursued self-destruction. When I could've been growing in knowledge and exceling academically, I dropped out of high school. And though I'd accepted Christ as my Savior at a young age, nearly a decade before my rather unglamorous behavior, my life was characterized by anything but faith.

In fact, I'm certain, had most of my adult friends encountered me during my teen years, they would've crossed to the other side of the street. Perhaps even talked among themselves about "that kind of girl."

The Shame I Carried

As an adult, fearing rejection, I kept my story hidden for decades. I was convinced if others knew what a mess I'd once been, they'd want nothing to do with me. And yet, overriding my regret and shame arched deep gratitude and awe for all God had done. Yes, my past demonstrated a life gone wrong, but more importantly, it revealed a life transformed.

I understood this, and at times, was brought to tears when I considered God's miraculous intervention. Oh, how I wanted to proclaim it all, if only so that others could see, through my testimony, His power, love, and grace!

One day, I shared my story with a friend I thought might understand, and perhaps even celebrate God's goodness revealed in me. That's far from what happened. A look of disgust passed across her face before she managed to adopt an appropriate "Christianese" smile and offer all the obligatory, "Praise God!" statements.

She then promptly showed me to the door. Rejection followed as she began to distance herself from me. Granted, I may have misread her behavior. Perhaps her life suddenly and coincidentally had grown too busy for get-togethers and returned phone calls. Maybe the depth of my shame, which God was just beginning to heal, colored my perception.

I'm sure there was some of that as it can be crazy-hard, especially in the beginning of our identity shifts, to separate reality from our interpretations of it. Regardless, I didn't share my story again for another three or so years, and only then because God made it clear, with numerous confirmations, that He wanted me to.

Moving Toward Emotional Freedom

When I finally obeyed, I felt ready to vomit, and my voice trembled so badly, I'm surprised anyone could decipher anything I said. My emotions—anxiety, fear, shame, gratitude, love for Christ, and surrender—were so jumbled, I ended my story in tears.

Later, I shared the experience with my brother, and he made a statement I've thought about many times since: "I look forward to the day you can share your story without shame."

I'm grateful to say, that day has come. Though I still feel twinges of fear, on occasion, when discussing my teen years, my former shame is now replaced by reverence, awe, and joy. Not just for all God did for me, but even more so for all the ways He wants to use my testimony to bring freedom to others—people bent on self-destruction or consumed with their own regrets and shame.

Freedom From Self

The more I focus on myself—my past, failures and regrets, and other people's judgments or perceptions of me—the more my insecurities grow and the more enslaved I become to each of those things. When I focus on Christ and His redemptive story, told not only through the pages of Scripture, but through my life as well, I experience peace, confidence, and unshakable freedom.

Our lives aren't ultimately about us, but what God wants to do in and through us. Don't misunderstand; God loves us deeply and receives joy from our joy, but His purposes extend far beyond that. Our faithlessness reveals His faithfulness, our failings His perfection, and our weaknesses His strength. Our momentary disappointments, as painful as they may be, are intended to point us toward those things this world can never give or take away—life eternal and unhindered access to Himself.

As you saw with my story, and as we'll see with Sarah's, in God's hands, our greatest "failures" can become powerful testimonies to His love and grace. Have you experienced that? Have you turned to Him for freedom—spiritual and emotional? If not, I hope you sense His heart for you. Through this study, He's drawing you closer and revealing Himself to you.

He's revealing how you too can move from shame to freedom and from merely surviving to experiencing the "filled to overflowing" life only He can give.

We've already discussed how barrenness was one of Sarah's most defining characteristics. Imagine being introduced by your greatest failure! And yet, based on our previous discussion, why might her story begin with this rather significant detail?

We'll see later how God met her in the middle of her pain, in her lack, and at her point of "failure," and used it all to reveal the power of His love and grace.

God has a way of doing that with all of us, if we let Him.

Read 1 Timothy 1:12-17.

What was Paul, the author of this passage, like before he knew Christ?

Notice the words, "But for that very reason" (NIV), "But … so that" (NLT), "But … for this reason" (ESV), or similar phrasing. What do these phrases point to?

How did Paul's past as a violent, blasphemous sinner reveal God's mercy and grace?

If you were rewriting that passage based on your story, how might it read? (Note: Not everyone has a dramatic "come to Jesus" moment, but if we belong to Him, we can all share our "before and after" scenarios, whether centered on who we were before our conversion, or perhaps who we were before a major growth moment.)

According to verse 16, Paul's life was intended to be an example to whom?

What was Paul's life an example of?

In what ways can your life provide the same example?

How might shifting your focus from your past, failures, or mistakes and onto the story God is writing through you help you move from shame and regret to confidence and praise?

Why might this shift require a moment-by-moment choice?

Do you believe you have the power, in Christ, to make this choice? (You may want to read 1 Peter 1:3 and 2 Corinthians 5:17.)

Close your study time by prayerfully thanking God for rewriting your story and redefining your name.

Day Five: The Battle for Truth, Hope, and Life
Review: Genesis 11:27-30
Read: Ephesians 2:1-13

Each day, we face three intense and relentless battles—that of truth over deception, vitality over despair, and hope over hopelessness. We gain or lose ground with every thought we entertain or discard. Scripture reveals the importance of demolishing all falsehood, taking our thoughts captive (2 Corinthians 10:5), and fixing our minds on truth. According to Romans 12:2, transformation comes when we renew our minds. As we yield to the power of the Holy Spirit and learn, meditate on, and choose to believe what we read in Scripture, areas of deception are replaced by truth.

This process seems easy in theory, but it's the application that proves difficult. For some reason, we give that little nagging voice within power over us. We focus on the unfounded and downright false rather than everything God says about us.

Training Our Minds

The more we give in to negative thinking, the more apt we are to do so. This has to do with what scientists call neuroplasticity, which refers to the way thoughts, behaviors, and actions restructure the human brain. Our thoughts develop ruts in our brains, known as neuronal connections, so that repeated mental states, ways of processing things, and ways of behaving become habit.

In other words, the more we focus on truth, the easier it becomes to do so in the future. Similarly, the more we focus on and feed the lies, the stronger they become and the more defeated we feel.

But in Christ, we have everything we need to live victoriously! We simply need to develop new habits—godly neuronal connections. By reading and meditating on Scripture, we can begin today!

Read Ephesians 2:1-13.

As you read, underline, highlight, or make note of words and phrases that stand out to you.

Why did those words or phrases resonate?

According to verse 1, what main characteristic defined you prior to Christ?

Consider life apart from Christ. How does spiritual death reveal itself in one's day-to-day interactions, behavior, and relationships?

How did Christ change you (v. 5)?

What are some characteristics of life in Christ?

Scripture often uses the imagery of light and darkness. In what ways was your life before Christ, or when you weren't living in obedience to Him, characterized by darkness?

How has God brought light to previously dark areas?

Make a table with two columns. Label the left-hand column "Before Jesus" and the right-hand column "After Jesus." Then, reread today's Ephesians passage and make note in the left column of how you behaved when you lived apart from Him. (If you received salvation at a young age, then note what your life would've looked like apart from Him.) In the right column, list who you are in Christ today.

Take a moment to pray, thanking Jesus for working in your life. Ask Him to continue moving you from fear to faith and despair or discouragement to a life overflowing with joy and peace.

Week Two:
An Unshakable Security

Jennifer Slattery
Day 1, 2
Susan Aken
Day 3, 4, 5

Order of completion:

<u>Large Group time:</u>

- Discuss the previous week's lessons on pages 3-19 and share anything that resonated with you or surprised you in the reading.

- Watch Becoming His Princess Week Two: Unshakable Security Video found on the Wholly Loved Ministries' YouTube channel (Search YouTube + Wholly Loved).

- Discuss the video as a group using the discussion questions on pages 23-24.

<u>Home lessons:</u>

- Day one: Choose one of the 2 options provided (p. 25 and 26).

Complete the remaining week's lessons as provided.

Week Two: An Unshakable Security
Viewer & Group Discussion Guide
From the Video:

Obedience always results in _____ with our Savior.

Surrender leads to increased _____ and _____.

We can't rest securely in God's _____ until we've learned to rest securely in _____.

With every encounter, we're either growing in _____ or in _____ to fear. We're either increasing in _____ or in _____, in _____ or _____.

Jesus said, "Now this is eternal life: that they _____ You, the only true God, and Jesus Christ whom You have sent" (John 17:3).

God is:

Jehovah-Shammah, the Lord who is _____ (Ez. 48:35).

El Roi, the God who _____ (Gen. 16:13).

Jehova-Jireh, the One who _____. (Gen. 22:14)

Jehova-Rapha, the God who _____ (Ex. 15:26).

El Olam, the _____ God (Gen. 21:33).

Group Discussion Questions:
Note to leaders: You probably won't have time to get to all the questions. Please let the discussion guide you, and focus on those questions you feel most beneficial to your group members.

What stood out to you, challenged you, stirred questions, or resonated with you as you read last week's passages and why?

What resonated with you most from today's video and why?

Think of a time when you moved, whether permanently or temporarily. What fears or concerns did you experience or struggles did you face?

Can you share a time when you sensed God asking you to leave something, be it a situation, friend group, or perhaps your home or job? What made this challenging? Did anything help you feel more comfortable or find courage to move forward?

Can you share a time when your obedience led to increased intimacy with Jesus or perhaps helped you know or understand God in a deeper way?

In what ways do we know God intellectually (through head knowledge)?

In what ways do we come to know God experientially (through experience)?

Why are both ways of knowing Him important?

Can you share a time when you came to know, through experience, God as your provider, healer, the One who is near, or the God who sees?

Day One (Option One)
Understanding God's Story
Read Genesis 12:1-9

Who are the main characters in this passage?

What does this passage reveal about the human condition, such as:
- Mankind's rebellion against/obedience toward God?

- Mankind's attempts to fill their needs apart from Him or relying on Him for their needs?

- Mankind's attempts to reach Him on their own terms?

What does this passage reveal regarding God's nature?

What does this passage reveal about God's plans?

How might this passage reveal mankind's need for the gospel?

In what ways are you/have you been similar to one or more of the characters in this passage?

What might God want you to know through this section of Scripture?

What might He be asking you to do?

End your reading in prayer, asking God to help you apply His word, recorded in Scripture, and live out whatever you sense Him impressing on your heart.

Day One (Option Two)
Bible Study Application Tool: Fact Versus Assumption
Read: Genesis 12:1-9

Early in my faith journey, I had a very shallow, subjective view of Scripture. In many ways, I made myself God by behaving as if I had authority over the Bible's message. When I read each day, I came to the text with preconceived ideas and an agenda. As a result, the "truths" I gleaned mirrored my heart more than God's. I didn't do this on purpose. I simply didn't know how to study Scripture. I wasn't alert to my tendency to read ideas and assumptions into the text. I certainly didn't know how to practice good Bible study application skills.

I "cherry picked" and followed my feelings. My favorite method—to randomly open my Bible, plop my finger somewhere on the page, and let the words "speak to me."

As a result, I misread and misunderstood a lot! I was practicing what Bible teachers refer to as an eisegetical approach to Scripture, which is basically a subjective interpretation based on one's previously held ideas or beliefs. This often occurs when someone uses a particular passage or verse to support their ideas, such as when an abusive husband quotes Ephesians 5:22, found in a passage commanding mutual submission, to oppress his wife.

Though I never used my faulty interpretation methods to mistreat others, I did, on occasion, use them to support a particular point. Like I said, this wasn't intentional; I simply hadn't been taught how to interpret Scripture properly.

And I'm not alone. We've all seen countless others handle God's Word in the same way. This results in vastly different and highly subjective interpretations, all in the name of truth. This mishandling of God's Word also leads to the proliferation of false teachings, erroneous beliefs, and division within the church.

Granted, we're a flawed people, and as a result, often arrive at flawed conclusions. Thankfully, God makes the crucial truths, like the gospel, clear and repeats them again and again. Knowing this gives me peace as I approach some of the more confusing parts of Scripture, and I hope it does you as well.

We need to begin by recognizing our reliance on previously held assumptions. All of us bring background knowledge and experiences to the text. Learning to separate Scriptural fact from assumption can help us decrease this error.

That's what we're going to be practicing today.

Before we can determine God's intended meaning for a passage, we must determine what the text says.

Review Genesis 12:1-10 and list all your observations. Note, these are simply facts without conclusions.

For example, in verse 1, I might list:
1. God spoke to Abraham.
2. God told Abraham to leave:
    a. His country.
    b. His people.
    c. His father's household.
3. God told Abraham to go:
    a. To an undisclosed land.
    b. A land that God would show him.
4. God promised to bless Abraham by:
    a. Making him into a nation.
    b. Making his name great.
5. God would protect/advocate for Abraham by:
    a. Blessing those who bless him.
    b. Cursing those who curse him.

This may seem tedious, but it's an important part of allowing the text to speak for itself.

Things Not Stated

For example, based on today's reading, what did God say to Sarah? What did Abraham say to Sarah? Did she want to leave Ur or did she have no choice? Does Scripture indicate the blessing given to Abraham would include her as well?

This leads to our second step in separating fact from assumption. As you list your observations, write down the questions that arise. If the question zips through your head, even if you think you don't have time to find the answer, write it down. You never know where that inquiry will lead. At the very least, it will help you zero in on what hasn't been stated. As we've discussed, this is important to clarify when studying God's Word.

God says what He wants, how He wants, when He wants to convey a message He wants us to hear. Our goal is to uncover that message to the best of our abilities and to align our lives with it.

As you end your reading in prayer today, ask God to help you do just that. Ask Him to help you apply what you've read and live out whatever He impressed on your heart.

Day Two
Bible Study Application Tool: Historical/cultural Context
Review: Genesis 12:1-9

Last week, we began our study by researching the backgrounds of the author of our text (Genesis) and his original or immediate audience (the ancient Hebrews during the time of the Exodus).

Now we move on to the historical and cultural context of the recorded narrative. For Genesis 12:1-9, this involves the time period during which Abraham and Sarah lived. Scholars generally place this narrative sometime during the "late third millennium BCE"[3] in ancient Mesopotamia. Ur had a rich cultural environment with a well-developed understanding of mathematics, literature, and astronomy. These people weren't dummies, intellectually speaking, but they were heavily deceived spiritually. Mythology, superstition, and the resulting fear and uncertainty dominated their thinking.

God called Abraham and Sarah out of this environment, brought them to Himself, and slowly transformed their theology from one that was subjective and works-based to one centered on grace. God also called them from a pagan background, where a plethora of false gods were worshiped, to a life centered on the one true God, their Creator.

To see the full beauty of this, we first need to understand the full depravity from which God plucked Sarah.

What questions might you formulate to help guide your research? List at least ten.

For example, you might ask:
What gods did the people of Mesopotamia worship?
What did their religious rituals look like?

What else might deepen your understanding of Sarah's cultural and (presumed) religious background? If you're not sure, you may find it helpful to brainstorm various roles she may have held and social arenas she may have occupied.

For example:
Wife
Bride
Woman
Housewife
Daughter

Scholars believe Abraham was wealthy. Though we don't know if Sarah was prior to her marriage, we can assume Abraham's wealth impacted her in some way. (You may find it interesting to research "bride auctions.")

---

[3] Feldman, Steven. "Biblical History: From Abraham to Moses, c. 1850-1200 BCE. COJS
http://cojs.org/biblical_history-_from_abraham_to_moses-_c-_1850-1200_bce-Steven_feldman-_cojs/

When I conducted my research, I investigated the gods and goddesses of Ur, the rights and roles of women in ancient Mesopotamia, childbearing, laws governing ancient Mesopotamian domestic life, and more. Each historical nugget I found deepened my understanding of today's passage and helped me consider the experiences, challenges, fears, and dreams Sarah may have held.

The further one goes back in time, the more challenging it is to locate credible and certain information. As a result, you'll probably find varying opinions and contradictory conclusions. Please don't let this confuse or frustrate you. Rather, remember that only the words of Scripture are wholly reliable. We can glean information from archaeologists and historians, but must remember, their interpretations arise from their observations, understandings, and personal leanings.

Here's a beautiful truth: The subjective nature of human wisdom deepens our respect for the unwavering and ever-certain truths presented in Scripture.

Let's review our goals and questions (as discussed last week):

1. Determine the original intended meaning. (What did the text mean at the time it was written?)
2. How were the original audience and/or biblical characters' cultures different from ours?
3. How were the original audience and/or biblical characters' cultures similar to ours?
4. What theological principle(s) are revealed through this narrative or passage?
5. Litmus test: Is the discovered principle consistent with the overall message and truths presented in Scripture?
6. How does that principle apply today, specifically, to me personally?

Day Three: Shaken Securities
Read: Genesis 12:1-9; 1 Peter 3:5-6; John 10:27-28; Luke 18:28-30

Sobbing, I (Susan) clung to my mother. With a goodbye, I walked out the door with a broken heart.

I was the daughter who would always stay close. Except for college, I lived at home until the age of twenty-nine. My family assumed I'd be the last to move out of state. Then my husband of three years asked me to pray about relocating to his home state of Nebraska. Though I did, I was sure I'd never choose to leave.

God spoke to my heart, "Will you trust Me, Susan? Will you say, 'I'm going?'"

When God speaks, He gives us the grace to follow.

I responded, "Yes Lord, I do trust You. I'm going to Nebraska. I'll go in my heart and in my will."

When Obedience Hurts

It was one of the most difficult choices I've made. I thought of all I'd miss once we moved. Knowing that I'd only see my family once or twice a year, I calculated how many more times I'd visit them.

I left behind my mom and dad and sisters. Nieces and nephews would grow up without me there. We said goodbye to a church we loved and close friends.

This was before texting, Face Time, or Skyping. At that time, we had letters or expensive long distance phone calls. Yes, we'd be near my husband's family, but I didn't know them well yet. Everything else was an unknown.

Even more daunting, we'd go without financial security. I gave up a teaching job of nine years while my husband was separating from the military. We didn't know when or where we would find employment or financial stability in Nebraska.

Sarah's Emotional Challenges

When Abraham told Sarah they'd be leaving family and friends to move to a distant land, he didn't ask her opinion. Her only choice was to go or be left behind. I imagine she shared some of my feelings. She had to say goodbye to her relatives knowing she would probably never see them again. There'd be no phone calls, no summer visits, and no mailman delivering letters.

She hugged her closest friends, aware they would never have another chat over the fire. She left the security of familiar surroundings for the unknown, safety of a household for exposure to foreigners, and assurance of her daily routine for the uncertainties of travel. She left what was usual for what was alien. She obeyed and followed her husband, but I think her heart may have been breaking as mine was.

Read Luke 18:28-30. Peter, one of Jesus' close followers, reminded Jesus that he and the other disciples had left everything to follow Him. With what promise did Jesus encourage Peter?

How does this promise encourage you?

What step do you need to take in order to obey Christ?

End your study time in prayer, asking God to show you where your trust in Him needs to grow and how you can cooperate with Him as He grows your faith.

Finding Security in Christ

Sometimes God calls us to leave behind people or places that have been our security, and we [are] shaken. When we step out in faith to obey, we learn He was our real security all along.

Faith is trusting that God is good even when obeying Him hurts. When we lose the earthly th[ings] we've placed our security in, we find the most important thing remains—our relationship [with] Christ.

Read Genesis 12:1. Describe the three areas in which Sarah encountered loss.

Which of these would be the most difficult for you to leave behind?

According to 1 Peter 3:5-6, where did Sarah find the courage to follow Abram? Who did she h[ope] in?

What challenges did she face? (List all you can think of.)

Describe a time when your faith in God gave you courage to trust completely in Him.

What promises did God give to Abraham in Genesis 12:2-3?

If Abraham shared with Sarah God's promise to bless him (and he may have) how do you think th[is] may have helped her feel secure as they journeyed into the unknown?

What promise did Jesus make to believers in John 10:27-28?

How can that promise help you when your sense of security is shaken?

Day Four
Choosing Faith

Review: Genesis 12:1-9
Read: Hebrews 11:1-3, 6,13-16 and 39; 1 Peter 1:3-9; Ephesians 1:3-14

When I followed God's leading to Nebraska, I didn't know what would happen. There was no guaranteed outcome. For months, I grieved over leaving my family, friends, and church. We lived with my mother-in-law at first because we had no jobs. We stored all our household goods in her garage. Once, after several storms, we discovered a leak in the garage. We'd packed everything in so tightly, it wasn't possible to know if anything was damaged.

In that moment, fearing I could lose everything, I examined my heart to see where my trust lay.

I wrote this in my journal: *"Does one material thing make a difference in me, or am I the same no matter what comes or goes? Is my heart at rest when the things I love might be lost? As I watch them go, I sense my heart is whole. They have no part of my soul. My soul is in Christ. His grace is my prize. Lasting joy comes from what is eternal and can never be lost."*

Was my security in my stuff? The people I left behind? A home of my own? Or was I trusting in Almighty God who sees everything from the beginning to the end and holds it all in His hands? Was He sufficient for me?

Faith means trusting Him even when I can't see Him, and I don't know what tomorrow will bring. I trust in who He is, not in my circumstances.

I imagine Sarah had doubts as she left Ur, and then again when she left Haran. Did God really call her and her husband on this journey? Would He provide for them, or would she and Abraham die of hunger and thirst? With every step she took away from her homeland and further into the wilderness, if Sarah looked at her circumstances, it would have been difficult to believe they made the right choice. But she kept trusting and following. If she'd caught a glimpse into the future, she would have seen that eventually her greatest wish would come true. But she reached that point by faith.

Similarly, if I'd known early in my marriage all God would do in my life and how He'd give me many of my heart's desires, I never would have doubted.

Read 2 Corinthians 5:7. How does God want us to live?

If we always knew the outcome of every choice, our faith wouldn't grow. We learn God is trustworthy by trusting Him and acting on our faith.

Read Hebrews 11:1-3 and 6. How do we display our faith?

To discover the reward this passage refers to, read 1 Peter 1:3-9. List all the rewards for faith you find.

When we seek God in belief, He allows us to know Him. He is our reward. He rewards us with His presence, His love, His peace, and His Spirit in our hearts. The things of this world are nothing. All that is physical is transient. The greatest benefits are eternal.

How can those eternal rewards give you security when everything else feels uncertain?

Read Hebrews 11:13-16, 39.

Did the heroes of the faith (including Sarah) receive all that they were promised while they lived on the earth?

What were they looking to as their reward?

These heroes had to look forward to the coming of Christ and their reward in heaven. We can look back knowing Christ came, and we have the privilege to read His words in Scripture. His Spirit lives in us. It's true our ultimate reward will come in heaven, but right now we have:

Peace in pain.
Comfort in sorrow.
Hope when all seems lost.
The ability to love.
His Spirit to empower us.
Grace lavished on us.

Read Ephesians 1:3-14. What other blessings can you find?

Write a prayer based on 1 Peter 1:3-9 thanking God for all He has given you through Jesus Christ.

Day Five: True Security
Read: Psalm 4:8; Matthew 6:19-21 and 25-34; Romans 8:35-39

"Be careful!"

I grew up with this motto. My mom so ingrained caution into my mind that I never made one trip to the emergency room. Never had a broken bone or stiches. But I also didn't learn how to swim, play sports, or do much of anything considered risky. She wanted to keep me safe.

We often equate security with being free from harm or the threat of danger. Don't we all want that? That's why we lock our doors, buy security systems, visit the doctor annually, hire policemen, and recruit military. We wear our seat belts, take our vitamins, purchase homes in a safe neighborhood, and take shelter during storms.

Proverbs 14:16 says, "The wise fear the LORD and shun evil, but a fool is hotheaded and yet feels secure." It's smart to choose safety instead of reckless abandon. But does our security rest in our wise choices? Does it depend on us?

What makes you feel secure?

Is there anything we can do that can guarantee our safety? Why or why not?

What can be secured?

God often calls us to leave what feels like security in order to obey Him. Do we ever leave real security behind to obey God? Explain.

In the Old Testament, Israel's second king, David, often faced danger. We can read his emotions and prayers during this time in the many Psalms he wrote. Read Psalm 4:8, a passage written by him. Based on his prayer, where did David place his security?

"In peace I will lie down and sleep." The Hebrew word for peace here is "shalom." It means a complete peace or wholeness, knowing the Infinite God, who is holy and perfect, covers us. This peace isn't dependent on circumstances but on knowing who God is. Max Lucado writes, "Faith is not the belief that God will do what you want. Faith is the belief God will do what is right.[4]" We are secure because we know, ultimately, we can trust God to do what is best in light of eternity.

In "shalom"—in wholeness, being held in His hands where no one can take me away—I will lie down and sleep, knowing whatever happens, He will make all things right. He is never absent, out-of-control, or at risk.

Read Matthew 6:33-34. Knowing we have no guarantee of another hour or day of life, how should we respond?

Read Romans 8:35-39. So much in life is uncertain. What can we hold onto with absolute certainty?

I seek to make wise choices. I don't want to be foolish or reckless. But if I refuse to take risks when following God's leading, my perception is wrong. I may think that I keep safe by avoiding exposure, but the truth is, I don't have that power.

God is my only security no matter where I go or what I do. We discover this as we journey through our lives. Sarah learned this lesson, as you will read about in coming weeks. God was her protector as He is ours.

That doesn't mean there isn't a cost to following Jesus. Stepping out to obey our Lord usually requires sacrifice; but if we refuse to step out in faith, we're holding onto cotton candy when He wants to give us eternal bread.

Take a moment to prayerfully seek God's will. How is He calling you to step out in faith?

Read or write out Romans 8:37-39, substituting your name where appropriate. Claim the truth of these verses for yourself.

---

[4] Lucado, Max. (1999) He Still Moves Stones. Thomas Nelson: Nashville, TN

Week Three
Remaining Faithful Through Disillusionment

Jennifer Slattery
Day 1, 2
Cheri Cowell
Day 3, 4, 5

Order of completion:

<u>Large Group time:</u>

- Discuss the previous week's lessons on pages 25-36 and share anything that resonated with you or surprised you in the reading.

- Watch Becoming His Princess Week Three: Remaining Faithful Through Disillusionment Video found on the Wholly Loved Ministries' YouTube channel (Search YouTube + Wholly Loved).

- Discuss the video as a group using the discussion questions on pages 39 and 40.

<u>Home lessons:</u>

- Day one: Choose one of the 2 options provided (p. 41 and 42).
    - If you chose option one for week two, read the passage in a different Bible translation this time and journal instead of repeating the questions.
- Complete the remaining week's lessons as provided.

Week Three
Viewer & Group Discussion Guide
From the Video:

Disillusionment comes whenever something we _____ doesn't _____ or things don't turn out as we _____.

Disillusionment can _____ or _____ Him.

Disillusionment can cause us to _____ or _____ our _____ and perceptions to _____.

Disillusionment can lead us to search for _____ fillers or the One who can fill us _____.

God is in the _____ and the _____, the _____ and the _____.

Disillusionment shifts our perspective off of _____ circumstances and _____ pleasures and accomplishments and onto the things of _____.

Disillusionment teaches us to focus on _____ rather than results.

The moment we take that first step of _____, we can call it a win and should _____ it.

Disillusionment teaches us to hold all things, other than Jesus, _____.

Group Discussion Questions:
Note to leaders: You may not have time to get to all the questions. Please let the discussion guide you, and focus on those questions you feel most beneficial to your group members.

What is your definition of success? Do you believe this when it comes to yourself?

What lies do you tell yourself regarding your calling, your relationship with God, your circumstances, and your abilities or responsibilities?

Are your obstacles more outside or inside?

What is preventing you from following God wholeheartedly and saying yes to the calling He's placed on your life?

How can reminding yourself of God's loving during periods of disillusionment help you remain strong and hopeful?

Why is it important to trust in God's timing?

Day One (Option One)
Understanding God's Story
Read Genesis 12:1-10

Who are the main characters in this passage?

What does this passage reveal about the human condition, such as:
- Mankind's rebellion against vs. obedience toward God?

- Mankind's attempts to fill their needs apart from Him vs. relying on Him for their needs?

- Mankind's attempts to reach Him on their own terms?

What does this passage reveal about God's nature?

What does this passage reveal about God's plans?

How might this passage reveal mankind's need for the gospel?

In what ways can you relate to one or more of the characters in this passage?

What might God want you to know through this section of Scripture?

What might He be asking you to do?

End your reading in prayer, asking God to help you apply His word and live out whatever you sense Him impressing on your heart.

Day One (Option Two)
Bible Study Application Tool: Sentence Analysis
Review: Genesis 12:1-10

Materials needed:
1. Pens/markers/colored pencils/crayons in the following colors:
   - Red
   - Green
   - Yellow
   - Orange

2. Genesis 12:1-10 copied from Biblegateway.com, pasted into a word document, double spaced, then printed out. (For today's lesson's purposes, I suggest using the NIV.)

Remember diagraming sentences in middle school grammar class? For those of you who wondered when or why you'd ever use those skills in real life, here's good news! While reading your Bible, you can once again practice analyzing and diagraming sentences. Syntax (word usage and placement) is vital to understanding the meaning of a sentence and the emphasis of a passage, as are other literary constructions we may have learned in school.

Let's look at some of those key elements now.

Conjunctions:

For example, words like "therefore," "since then," "so that," and "because" connect one part of a sentence to another. Our first goal is determining what idea or passage those words point to. For example, Colossians 3 begins with, "Since, then, you have been raised with Christ …" This suggests Paul is developing his statement in this chapter based on points discussed in Colossians 2. To fully understand his message, then, we need to read the words leading up to it.

On your printed page of Genesis 12:1-9, underline every conjunction (including subordinating—those, like "in" that join independent and dependent clauses) in green.

What do the "ands" used in verses 1-3 tell you? (In what ways are the promises revealed related? Do they show conditions or contrasts?)

What does the "so" in verse 4 point back to?

What does the "so" in verse 7 refer to?

What does the "because" in verse 10 connect or point to?

We don't see any "buts" in today's text. If we had, they would show a contrast. For example, Romans 6:23 says, "For the wages of sin is death, **but** the gift of God is eternal life in Christ Jesus our Lord." The result of sin is contrasted with God's gift, and death is contrasted with life.

Cause-and-Effect Relationships:

Read through the text again, this time looking for a stated cause and effect. Underline these in red. Sometimes these will be revealed using conjunctions, but not always.

Did you notice the cause-and-effect relationship between verses 1-3 and 4? What about within the first part of verse 3? What about in verse 7?

Now look at 6:23? What is the cause in that verse? What is the effect?

Look for lists:

Do you see any lists in Genesis 12:1-9? Star each item in the list. (For example, you'll find one in verses 1-3, and another in verse 5.)

Setting Clues:

Underline words that indicate chronology, time, and location in yellow. For example, "At that time," lets us know when the Canaanites lived in the land, and "then" in verse 9 tells us Abraham left after doing what verse 8 describes. Though these time hints may not appear to offer much insight in regard to today's text, they can greatly impact our understanding of other Bible passages. Therefore, it's helpful to develop the habit of remaining alert to all words and statements that help us understand when certain events occurred.

Actions:

Circle all verbs in the passage in red and then determine if the verb is:
Active or passive (Often, passive verbs are connected with helping and being verbs: was, is, have been, etc.)
Past, present, or future
Imperative (God's command)

For example, in verse 1, we learn God will directly make Abraham into a nation, *will bless* him, and *will make* his name great. These are active and future. We also learn Abraham *will be* a blessing, which is passive and future. Abraham doesn't have to do anything. The blessing will happen *to* him.

Pronouns:

Circle all pronouns in green and then make note of to whom the pronoun refers. For example, in verses 1-3, "I" refers to God. We see God is the one who will do the blessing.

Repeated words and phrases:

In orange, circle repeated words, first in each particular sentence, then in the passage overall, and draw a line to connect them. Circle repeated phrases in orange also, and draw a line to connect them. In today's passage, this doesn't happen often, but I find one phrase in particular significant.

Idioms:

You won't find any idioms in today's text, but I wanted to mention them because it's always important to make note of figures of speech. For example, in Acts 26:14, when Saul is opposing Christ, Jesus tells him, "It is hard for you to 'kick against the goads.'" A goad was a pointed stick ancient herders used to prod animals to move in a particular direction. In response, sometimes the animals kicked the goad, causing the sharp end of the stick to prick their flesh. The more they kicked, the more pain they experienced.

Comparisons and similarities:

We don't see a lot of comparisons and similarities, if any, in today's text. But we still want to be alert to any ideas, people, or things that are compared or similar to one another.

As you evaluated today's passage, did any questions arise? If so, I encourage you to jot them down in your journal for further study when you have time. Did any thoughts or new insights arise during today's lesson? Might God be emphasizing anything? What does the text reveal about God?

End your reading in prayer, asking God to help you apply His word and live out whatever you sense Him impressing on your heart.

Day Two
Bible Study Application Tool: Geological Context
Review: Genesis 12:1-10

We've been working to ground ourselves in Abraham and Sarah's time period and locations. First, we looked at the city of Ur, its culture, religion, and societal expectations. Next, we examined women's roles specifically—in marriage, motherhood, and societal value. Today, we're venturing into new territory. As Abraham and Sarah continue their travels, their environment, lifestyle, and encounters will change.

Honestly, you could spend days, if not weeks, researching the historical context of each weekly passage we cover. Though we don't have time for such in-depth analysis this go-around, I hope you'll return to this narrative when you do have sufficient time to implement all the Bible study tools you've learned more fully.

Review Genesis 11:27-32 and Genesis 12:1-10. Note locations mentioned (cities, rivers, mountains, kingdoms).

Find at least one location mentioned on a map. Most Bibles have maps in the back, but if yours doesn't, you can find some online. Search using the term "Abraham's Journey." You may also want to purchase a Bible Atlas or check one out from your local library.

As you read today's passage, what questions intrigue you regarding the geographical area Sarah and Abraham covered? List five to ten you could use for further study. (Do so before reading mine below.)

Here are mine:
(Please note, I won't research all of these. This is simply a list I can select from, and then I research based on my time availability. Don't allow this to overwhelm you. Instead, use it as a tool you can utilize as and when God leads.)

How long did it take Abraham and Sarah to get from Ur to Haran?
What was the terrain like?
How long did it take them to get from Haran to Shechem?
What was the terrain like?
How might the terrain have posed challenges?
How did they eat and drink along the way?
How difficult was their travel?
How did they feed their livestock? Was there plenty of pastureland along the route they took?
How populated was their route?
What kind of wildlife might they have encountered?
What unique challenges might the wildlife have posed?
What people groups might they have encountered along the way?
What was the land of Canaan like?
Where were the Canaanite borders?

Where specifically was Shechem?
What was Shechem like (agriculturally, in terms of terrain, population, and climate)?
Where was the oak of Moreh?
Where was the hill country?
What was the terrain of the hill country like?
What was each area they encountered or traveled through like agriculturally?
Where was Bethel?
Where was Ai?
Where is the Negev?
Are any of the above areas/locations mentioned elsewhere in Scripture, and if so, where?
Do any of the areas/locations mentioned above have special significance? If so, how?

Obviously, you won't have time to investigate all your questions, or mine, today. So perhaps choose one to research further. You may do so online and at a local library. If you have a seminary in your area, they will likely let you use books in the facility. Some may even allow you to apply for a library card and check resources out to take home.

As you get to know the land Sarah traveled across better, your understanding of her and how she might have felt will deepen.

You may want to close your study today journaling your thoughts (and any more questions you have) regarding what you've discovered.

End your research time in prayer, asking God what He wants to show you from today's lesson. Ask Him to remind you of His presence as you engage in your own journey.

Day Three
Problems in Paradise

Review: Genesis 12:4-10
Read: 1 John 4:4, 2 Thessalonians 3:3, Deuteronomy 31:6, Psalm 28:7-8

The storms that night were unusual. My husband, Randy, and I (Cheri) watched the news before going to bed: "Severe thunderstorms in our area with clear skies by morning," the weatherman said. Sleep came easily with that assurance. Randy left early for work, but called shortly after to tell me to turn on the news quickly, for all had not been well last night. Sketchy reports were coming in: three tornadoes had touched down in our town, quite a few people were found dead, and the destruction was widespread.

The news reporters were showing incredible pictures stating, " …and, some of the worst destruction has happened in Garden Grove[5] where at least two are dead and the number could rise." Later, forty-two were confirmed dead from three F4 tornados, and an estimated $16 million dollars of damage was done, mostly in poor neighborhoods.

"Oh, no, Lord! My church, my friends, my kids …"

Unmet Expectations

I had been the youth and children's ministry director for a church right in the heart of Mayberry—at least I thought of it that way when I landed the job. I had a degree in children's theatre, but had answered God's call into full-time ministry. At first all was perfect. I'd canvassed the neighborhood soon after I arrived and invited the kids that played basketball on the church property to join us for youth events.

I was excited, but soon discovered not all shared my enthusiasm for the growth of our programs. Parents began calling and asking why I was disciplining their child when those children were the troublemakers. Joy quickly became misery when these parents formed an alternative youth group at their homes—one with strict rules about who was invited. The teens wouldn't even sit on the same side of church as I did on Sunday mornings. Many days I sat in my office and cried, "Lord, why am I here? Why won't You let me quit?"

Somehow I persevered day after day with no other explanation except a desire to be obedient. I knew in the depth of my spirit I'd been called there, yet even my husband wanted me to quit. Still I stayed.

Pushing Through the Hard

Have you stepped out in faith believing you were called to go somewhere or do something only to be met with obstacles? Perhaps you, like me, had people within your family begging you to make a different choice, and yet you knew you were doing what God had asked of you.

---

[5] Name of town has been changed

What did God tell Abraham and Sarah to do in Genesis 12:1?

According to verse 4, how did they respond?

They went, after losing his father and his brother (Gen. 11:28, 32). In their old age, and still without a child of their own, which many assumed would represent God's blessings, they simply went.

Read Genesis 12:4-6. Who did they find when they got to this promised land?

That's right, the land wasn't empty and simply waiting there for them. The land was occupied by Canaanites. This people group is mentioned over 150 times in the Bible. They were a wicked, idolatrous nation descended from Noah's grandson Canaan, who was a son of Ham.

We're told that Abraham passed through the land of Canaan, no doubt having seen the temples for child sacrifice and other idolatrous behavior, and proceeded to the oak of Moreh.

Knowing Who to Rely On

When things aren't as you dreamed in the place where you've been called, is your first inclination to stop and dwell on the obstacle, or move through and seek godly wisdom? Sometimes I get it right and seek God first, and thankfully I'm learning to do that more and more. But sometimes I allow the obstacles to appear bigger than my God. I forget that if God has called me, He is with me.

Read 1 John 4:4. According to this verse, where does our confidence lie?

The only reason we stand in victory is because we stand in Jesus—or rather, He stands in us. If this were written into an equation, it might read: Victory comes from God who is > than any opposition in this world. Looked at in another way it may read: You + God > Satan + any opposition in this world. If John were writing this for you today he might say God is > than your car breaking down. God is > than you losing your job. God is > than a political world gone crazy. God is > worry, stress, anxiety, fear, or doubt. He is greater than any problem you may have. God is Greater. Period. And if you've trusted Jesus for salvation, He is in you!

How does that reality change the way you see your current difficulties?

Abraham saw the Canaanites in the land God had promised him, and instead of viewing that obstacle as too big, he went straight to his bigger God.

After the news report of tornados that morning I quickly dressed and headed for the church. As I got closer, dread enveloped me. What damage had been done? What about the youth and the families I worked with? Would they know how to find me? How would I find them? As quickly as the questions tumbled through my mind, the assurances from God quieted my spirit. My car became a sanctuary as the Holy Spirit met each fearful thought with a Scripture or memory of God's past faithfulness. By the time I reached the church I had a deep sense of His peace.

Read these Scriptures listed below and circle the one you will memorize so the next time an obstacle stands before you, God can remind you of His truths.

2 Thessalonians 3:3
Deuteronomy 31:6
Psalm 28:7-8

Day Four
Building Altars
Review: Genesis 12:4-10
Read: Matthew 8:23-27, Isaiah 26:3, Philippians 4:19, Romans 8:28-29, 1 Peter 5:10, Ephesians 2:10

I almost held my breath as I turned that final corner. There the church stood, all intact, so very peaceful. I soon found that a three-mile path of destruction had been wrought through an apartment complex, a retirement mobile home park, a migrant community, and then skipped over the neighborhood in which the church stood.

The church office was quickly filling with volunteers looking for direction. "What can I do?" I asked the pastor.

"Begin by calling these numbers and let me know what you find."

With the list of contacts I was soon immersed in a whirlwind of activity. Within twenty-four hours I found myself pulling together the volunteers and leaders of forty area churches of all denominations to help victims retrieve personal items from their piles of rubble, do house-by-house assessments of needs, and babysit so parents could apply for federal aid.

A week after that dark night, with great enthusiasm I jumped out of bed, ready to handle more tornado work. Suddenly, I realized I hadn't been miserable for a week. And then, as if a movie were passing before my eyes, I could see God's whole plan.

Grace-Based Understanding

I saw how God kept me in a job I really didn't like, in a place I wasn't really comfortable, and then placed me in a position for which I was completely unqualified—so I could be used by Him. The words in Proverbs 3:5-6 had new meaning, "Trust in the Lord with all your heart and lean not on your own understanding; in all your ways submit to Him, and He will make your paths straight" (NIV).

As the reality of God's handprint seeped into my heart, I began to cry. I called my pastor's wife and through sobs I said, "He wouldn't let me quit, because He needed me."

"What do you want me to do?" she asked.

"Just listen to me cry," I sobbed. "He was there the whole time and now I can see. He loves *me* and can use *me*."

That week I was named the director of what became Operation L.O.V.E. (Linking Our Volunteer Efforts), an ecumenical organization that connected tornado victims to the help they needed from the government and area agencies. If they didn't "qualify" for the official aid, Operation L.O.V.E. stepped in. We basically became a volunteer construction company, rebuilding and repairing over fifty-four homes and lives.

Genesis 12:7 tells us the Lord met Abraham at the oak in Shechem and confirmed His promises to him. Notice, God didn't remove the obstacles, but He confirmed His promises. Sometimes you and I are delivered from our situations, but more often than not God simply reminds us of His faithfulness while we endure. I went from one mess into a storm of a different kind. Yet, in the midst of each one, God showed me that He'd been with me the whole time.

Read Matthew 8:23-27.

What stands out to you most in this passage?

What does this passage reveal about God? (List all the divine attributes you find.)

If I were in the place of the disciples I would have done the same thing, wouldn't you? This story is repeated in Matthew, Mark, and Luke because it must have been a turning point in their faith.

The story tells us Jesus was with them in the boat. We also learn He can calm the storms on the Sea of Galilee, and we know from elsewhere in Scripture He calms storms in our lives. The story assures me that even if it looks like Jesus is asleep in my boat—seemingly unaware of the storm that is about to swamp my life—He is in control. He had me in the palm of His hand when I sat crying in my office at church, and He'd called me to be right where He could use me when the storm ceased. If I'd given up, turned back, or cowered in the face of opposition, I wouldn't have received the blessing of being a part of what God did there.

Abraham built an altar to the God who is faithful. You and I build an altar every time we give Him honor and glory for what He is able to do through us.

Every day during the two years that followed the tornado, I experienced His direct answers to prayers. One day I got off the phone with a lady who didn't qualify for help from any of the other social/civic organizations because her roof was already in bad shape before the tornado. Now she was eight months pregnant, and when it rained her home flooded. We had volunteers to repair the roof, but where were we going to get the new carpet? We circled up in prayer and said out loud, "God, You know the need, and if it be Your will to supply this carpet, Your will be done."

Within minutes a man knocked at our door saying, "We just finished a job and have this carpet. Could you use it?"

Day after day I watched God answer prayers in real and tangible ways, yet the greatest miracle to me was how God used me. With a gentle touch He helped me to hear His desire to stay at a place where I was unhappy and gave me the strength to hold on when all else told me to leave. Then He used every skill He had ever given me so that I was able to serve where no one else could.

Every time I share this story, I'm building an altar to my faithful God.

When have you stayed, endured, and later learned the why?

Looking back, how was God faithful, either while you were waiting, or in the midst of the storm?

What stories can you share that will build an altar to your faithful God?

He heard my heart's deepest desire—to know Him in a personal way and to be used by Him—and He met me there. There, among the rubble, He met me. He desires to meet you there, too. He is there in the storm and He's already in the boat with you.

If your heart's deepest desire is to be known and used by God, write a short prayer here expressing this desire.

Read the following verses and record what each one promises:

Isaiah 26:3

Philippians 4:19

Romans 8:28-29

1 Peter 5:10

Ephesians 2:10

Day Five
The Lies We Believe

Review: Genesis 12:4-10
Read: Galatians 6:9, 1 Corinthians 10:13, Philippians 2:4-7, 1 John 2:15-17, John 20:29, 2 Corinthians 12:9-10, Genesis 50:19-20

After my two years in disaster recovery work, it was time for a new career. I asked God to just open a door and shove me through it, because I was exhausted emotionally and mentally. And God did. I took a new youth and children's ministry job on the other side of town. My husband and I sold our house and bought a new one over there. I was determined to "keep my nose clean," as the saying goes.

There were a few things I didn't like, as there are with any job. One of those things was the pastor's habit of bringing me into his office and inviting me to join him in praying for a list of concerns. I was uncomfortable hearing what others had shared in private, but I figured those secrets were safe with me.

One day at a ladies Bible study I heard those prayers shared by someone else, but they weren't the same. Details were different. Someone wasn't telling the truth. Another staff member was present. Our eyes met and we knew—we both had been invited to hear private prayers. We learned other staff members were also asked to participate in these same types of prayers. As a staff we decided each of us would tell the pastor the next time we were invited to hear prayer concerns that God already knew the needs so we'd prefer not to hear the details.

A few months went by, and I was breathing a sigh of relief. But then a parent called crying, "Why did you tell him? Now I'm going to lose my children." This parent had only told the pastor and me about a secret that could harm her custody case, and now her ex-husband knew. I hadn't told anyone. Now I couldn't stay silent. I reported my concerns to my liaison on the pastor-staff relations board and within 24-hours I was fired and escorted from the building. On Sunday morning ten accusations were made against me—from the pulpit, including inappropriate conduct with children. As I sat in my car wailing and railing against God, I demanded to know why. Where was He? Didn't He see what I was going through?

Abraham and Sarah must have felt this way when they reached the land of Canaan. They'd been obedient. They'd left behind everything they knew and went somewhere that at first wasn't fully known. When they got there, the land was occupied. And then a famine hit. What gives?

It's said bad things come in threes, but in reality, sometimes they come in fours, fives, and sixes. Perhaps you've done what God has asked, and now it appears He's abandoned you. When this happens, we can question whether we heard God right in the first place. If we know God sent us, then we wonder if we are "out of God's will."

Both questions are based in lies.

Read the following Scriptures and write the truth revealed in each and a lie that truth counters. I've completed the first one as an example.

Galatians 6:9
Truth: Keep on, keeping on–Do the right thing and don't give up even when it is hard because the sowing season will eventually end, the harvest is guaranteed, and blessings are coming.

Lie: Surely the harvest would have come by now, I must not be doing the right things, sowing the right seed, be in God's will, or pleasing God–so give up now. It's not worth it.

1 Corinthians 10:13
Truth:

Lie:

Philippians 2:4-7
Truth:

Lie:

1 John 2:15-17
Truth:

Lie:

John 20:29
Truth:

Lie:

2 Corinthians 12:9-10
Truth:

Lie:

Genesis 50:19-20
Truth:

Lie:

God's Word always gives us the truth we need to combat all lies, but we must plant that truth in our hearts so we can use it to stop the lies from sending us off course. Choose one of these Scriptures that spoke to you today and take time to contemplate it this week. Tuck that truth in your heart so you can stand strong when the famine hits.

What lies have you allowed to hold you back or keep you rooted in fear or discouragement? Close your lesson time today in prayer asking God to show you what lies need to be replaced with truth.

Week Four:
Fear, Faith, & the God Who Saves

Jennifer Slattery

58

Week Four:
Viewer & Group Discussion Guide
From the Video:

Our fears and how we behave when afraid reveal what we truly believe about _____, and _____ and _____ to care for us.

Whenever we live _____ of _____ for us, we distance ourselves from Him—our source of love, hope, power, and life.

_____ robs us of the joy and peace filled life God promised us.

When confronted with a life-threatening situation, King Jehoshaphat's _____ was _____.

In Jehoshaphat's prayer, He reminded himself and the people of: _____.

_____.

_____.

_____.

_____.

It's never too late to _____, to take our thoughts _____, and _____ on truth.

Group Discussion Questions:
Note to leaders: You probably won't have time to get to all the questions. Please let the discussion guide you, and focus on those questions you feel most beneficial to your group members.

What stood out to you, challenged you, stirred questions, or resonated with you as you read last week's Bible passage and why?

What resonated with you most from today's video and why?

What are some common fears women face?

What do you tend to be afraid of, or when do you most tend to become afraid?

What truths regarding God (His character, past miracles He's performed, or His) counter that fear?

Which of the four divine attributes revealed in Jehoshaphat's prayer (God's sovereignty, power, presence, and attentiveness) bring you the most comfort and why?

When you're anxious or afraid, how readily do you turn to prayer?

How can praying when afraid help bring peace, courage, and freedom?

What does it mean to take one's thoughts captive?

Can you share a time when you were feeding anxious thoughts but then determined to focus on truth instead? What happened?

What are some other ways, when anxious or afraid, you shift your focus off your problems and onto God?

Each time you choose to do so, you'll be forming new neural pathways in your brain, which will make it easier to focus on truth in the future!

Day One (Option One)
Understanding God's Story
Read: Genesis 12:10-20

Who are the main characters in this passage?

What does this passage reveal about the human condition, such as:
- Mankind's rebellion against/obedience toward God?

- Mankind's attempts to fill their needs apart from Him or relying on Him for their needs?

- Mankind's attempts to reach Him on their own terms?

What does this passage reveal regarding God's nature?

What does this passage reveal about God's plans?

How might this passage reveal mankind's need for the gospel?

In what ways are you/have you been similar to one or more of the characters in this passage?

What might God want you to know through this section of Scripture?

What might He be asking you to do?

End your reading in prayer, asking God to help you apply His word and live out whatever you sense Him impressing on your heart.

Day One (Option Two)
Bible Study Application Tool: Investigating Original Words
Read: Genesis 12:10-20

Because language is constantly changing and adapting to culture, it's helpful to look up the meaning of the original word used in a particular verse. Words that meant something in, say, the 1200s and 1300s, may now communicate something drastically different. For example, virtue once held the connotation of strength, courage, valor, and high moral character.

Now, however, when we think of virtue, our minds shift to propriety or modesty. This impacts how we read Proverbs 31:10, which says, "Who can find a virtuous wife ..." or, as the NIV reads, "A wife of noble character ..." The ESV calls her an excellent wife, and other translations call her capable and good. But none of these quite hit the original Hebrew, *chayil*, which can be defined as army, strength, efficiency, and wealth.

In other words, the woman described in Proverbs 31 has victorious, warrior-like qualities!

To find breakdowns of the original words, visit BibleHub.com and type one verse in the site's search bar. The verse will pull up in multiple translations. Above this, you will see "Hebrew" or "Greek," depending on which Testament your verse is in. (Most of the Old Testament was written in Hebrew, whereas the New Testament was written in Greek.) Next you'll see a list of words with numbers assigned on the far left. Click on the number; this will lead you to all the word's definitions (as one word often has numerous possible meanings) along with an indication of which meaning fits what verse based on context.

When you read Genesis 12:10-20, did any words stand out to you? Note five to ten words you can investigate further. I'm always intrigued by adjectives, so "severe" (v. 10), "serious" (v. 17), "beautiful" (vs. 11 and 14), and "very beautiful" captured my attention. I'm curious as to why the "very" was added and if the two English words arise from one Hebrew word. The NIV also says that Pharaoh's officials "praised" her to him, which intrigues me as well.

I especially enjoy looking up the original names for God. In verse 17, God is called the LORD. From what Hebrew word is this translated?

Where else is that name used for God?

Read three or four verses listed beneath this word. Do those verses increase or add anything to your understanding of God?

Verse 16 also piqued my curiosity. The NIV says Abraham "acquired" numerous things, including servants. My assumption has always been that the Pharaoh gave these items to him, but the text doesn't clearly reveal this. Unfortunately, the original Hebrew doesn't answer my question, but based on the context, I think it's safe to assume these items did come from Pharaoh.

I may also choose to investigate "inflicted" and "diseases" (v. 17).

Choose one of the words you want to study further using BibleHub or Blue Letter Bible. As you do, make note of any thoughts or questions that arise.

Did your understanding deepen through your research?

Today's passage may not have seemed to offer many intriguing words for further study, but like with all our Day One and Two lessons, the main point is to become comfortable using this Bible study application tool.

End your reading in prayer, asking God to help you apply His word and live out whatever you sense Him impressing on your heart.

Day Two
Bible Study Application Tool: Political Context
Review: Genesis 12:11-20

Throughout their travels, Sarah and her husband encountered numerous people groups, cultures, and political entities. They'd left their homeland of Ur (of the Chaldees), located in Mesopotamia, with its independent citystates and their patron deities, trekked through Canaan, and ultimately, to Egypt. Sometime you may want to research ancient Mesopotamia, the cultures and customs of the Canaanites (and how Abraham's erecting of an altar could've been viewed as a political threat), as well as nomadic living and everything related to that.

To keep our lessons manageable, however, I'm going to suggest you camp out in ancient Egypt for a while. You can find information on sites such as BibleHistory.com and biblearchaeology.org. Your local library also likely has numerous books on ancient Egypt that may not provide a biblical perspective but can help you understand the political backdrop when Abraham and Sarah visited the land.

Looking purely at their political influence, what questions might today's reading trigger? Write those down.

We always want to be alert to potential cultural differences between us, the writer, original audience, and cultures encountered. To that end, list questions that could help guide your research. For example, in what ways was the Pharaoh similar to and different from the priests who ruled over Mesopotamian citystates? In what ways was he similar to and different from our political structure? Did he have absolute or limited power? From where did his power ultimately derive?

Considering that wealth is also mentioned, you may want to research ancient Egyptian economics.

When I read Genesis 12:14-16, I was especially intrigued by questions relating to the Pharaoh's harem. How many women were normally taken into his palace? Where did they go or stay? Did they immediately enter into the Pharaoh's presence, or did they undergo a beauty regime similar to Esther's in the book bearing her name? Was Sarah slated to become the Pharaoh's wife (and to answer that question, you'd want to look up the original Hebrew word translated as "wife" here) or more of a concubine?

And why was Abraham afraid men would kill him for his wife? Was this common? Are there stories, perhaps in ancient writings, that could lend insight into this or his state of mind? How might the Pharaoh's power at this time play in to this? What might the modern-day equivalent be?

I'm also curious as to what's meant by the Pharaoh's "household."

What other questions arise relating to Egypt's leader, economics, or leadership structure? Choose one to research further. Then jot down some thoughts regarding how that deepens your understanding of Sarah's betrayal, fear, and vulnerability.

Day Three
Fighting Fear
Review: Genesis 12:11-20
Read: Hebrews 11:8-12

What are your three greatest fears? Mine almost always center on my family's well-being, my physical safety, and other people's opinions of me. And somewhere tied up within those three broader categories lie enough worries to keep my stomach tied up in knots indefinitely—if I let them.

When threatened, I'm tempted to respond in one of two ways—I react (sometimes A.K.A. as lash out), or I retract. Sometimes I do both. I've been known to go to great lengths—from driving across the country to avoid spending a few hours on a plane, to religiously cutting coupons and scouring grocery ads—in order to avoid my fears.

Most would recognize the root of my behavior in avoiding the airplane. My extreme budgeting, however, is more challenging to unpack. In fact, many young moms once found my practice admirable. An example of self-control.

They hadn't a clue how much my actions—and the emotions fueling them—were controlling me. My fears and pain from past experiences took healthy and wise behaviors and turned them into something that dominated and enslaved. I didn't want to just watch our budget. I wanted it balanced to the penny. A week's worth of food in the fridge and pantry wasn't enough; I needed both stocked to the brim. Had you opened my cupboards when we were living in Bossier City, Louisiana, you might have been shocked and amused to find eight or more jars of peanut butter, numerous boxes of cereal, and an abundance of other staples clogging my shelves.

We probably would've laughed while I pointed out how much I'd saved shopping for each. In other words, I would've offered a very reasonable explanation for my actions, one I actually believed, until God stirred things up a bit.

Getting to the Root

Past moves and my time on the streets of Tacoma created deep-seated fears within me—of hunger, of being vulnerable and getting hurt, of not having a steady and safe place to sleep …. although I didn't realize this at the time. I'd become quite adept at distracting myself and suppressing my emotions. What I *wasn't* so great at was learning to feel—so I could heal.

But God knew. Not only could He clearly see the root of all of my strange, slightly obsessive activities. He also knew where I'd land—emotionally, relationally, and mentally—if He didn't intervene. He understands the lasting impact our thoughts have on our mood, behaviors, and future thought processes.

I mentioned briefly how our brains are constantly rewiring themselves. We see this especially in regard to fear. When we're afraid of something and avoid that thing, our brains take this as proof that

that thing truly was dangerous. This is likely why our fears, anxieties, and obsessions get worse over time.

Have you heard the term "exposure therapy"? It's a treatment in which mental health professionals intentionally expose their patients to situations, activities, or items they fear in order to "normalize" them.

That's not a treatment plan I'd rush to sign up for, I can tell you that! I'm much more prone to the "keep that thing away from me and I'll be fine" route. (Also known as hiding, avoiding, and isolating.) In other words, I quickly allow my fears to control me.

Grace-Based Freedom

But Christ died to set us free—from sin and its devastating effects. Therefore, being the loving and merciful Father He is, He often performs the most drastic, painful, terrifying, and freeing therapy session our trembling brains can handle. For me, that involved my husband quitting his job, followed by a period of unemployment. This story will probably read somewhat familiar to you as I referenced in briefly in week three's audio and video segments. Honestly, I tend to reference it a lot because God taught me so much through that period. This situation resulted in us selling our home, cramming our belongings into our mini-van and storage lockers, and moving to a 500-square foot, rent-by-the-month apartment not knowing how long we'd be there or where we'd go next.

In other words, God allowed me to face one of my worst fears—financial insecurity—so that He could demonstrate His power over it. He remained in control over everything—our finances, the job market, me and my family, and our grocery bill.

Maybe you have a similar story. When I read Sarah's experience in Egypt, I wonder if perhaps God was doing the same with her. Was He allowing her to experience one of her greatest fears—being discarded and abandoned and left vulnerable, at the mercy of strangers—to initiate freedom through it?

God's Grace Revealed

Was God showing her He was bigger and stronger than anything she might face, even a powerful Pharaoh?

Pause to remember what we learned regarding how women were viewed in Sarah's culture—especially societal expectations and issues related to barrenness. If you had been in her position, what fears might you have experienced?

How secure do you think you would've felt in your marriage?

As she traveled further and further from Ur, I wonder if her anxieties lessened or grew.

If you had been in her situation, how do you think your emotions would've changed?

Had I been in her sandals, I probably would've peppered Abraham with questions: Are you sure you heard God? But He just said leave? Without telling you where to go or how long it'd take you to get there? That doesn't make sense. What if we missed the turn back at that bush back there?

What happened in Genesis 12:10?

Have you ever felt food insecure? If so, can you describe that feeling? If not, can you imagine how you might feel if your food source (income and grocery stores or perhaps farms) suddenly dried up?

We probably can't fully relate to how catastrophic famines were in ancient times. When we get fired or laid off, we can file for unemployment or visit a food bank. If a drought kills local crops, our country can ship produce in from elsewhere. If cattle were to die out for some reason, we could fulfill our protein needs through plant sources.

Abraham and Sarah didn't have those options, nor could they rely on family and friends because as Scripture reminds us, they were foreigners and nomads (Heb. 11). As we discussed in Week Two, with every step, God was removing those things in which they'd previously placed their security and was drawing them to Himself. And yet, if Sarah was anything like me, she simply shifted her security from the comforts and familiarity of Ur onto her husband, her provider and protector.

When Our Fears Become Reality

Until he failed her. Read Genesis 12:11-13. How would you have felt, if you'd been Sarah?

As she and her husband were about to enter a strange land filled with people they likely knew very little about, the man God had placed in her life to cherish and protect her says, in essence, "The men in this land are out of control. When they see you, your beauty will trigger animalistic, murderous behavior. There's no telling what they'll do! And here's the thing. I really don't want to die. Can you help me out? I know! How about if we tell them you're my sister?"

If there ever was a time when she felt disposable, worthless, and insecure, this was it. Did she try arguing with him, or was she too shocked, too broken, and maybe too terrified, to respond?

Though Scripture doesn't tell us what she thought, said, or felt, we can imagine how we might respond if someone were to betray us in a similar manner. Most of us probably would've been shooting desperate pleas heavenward, begging God to intervene—and maybe to knock some sense into our spouses! I probably would've reminded God that I hadn't wanted to leave Ur in the first place. Concluding my husband was to blame for our predicament, I may have viewed the famine and the events that followed as an indication that he hadn't heard God and was dragging me and our clan across the desert on some misguided whim gone horribly wrong.

When have you done that? What circumstances caused you to doubt your husband's leadership and decision-making? Or, if you're not married, think of a time when you were forced to trust someone you disagreed with or whose wisdom you questioned.

In this situation, do you feel Sarah would've been justified to do the same?

But what if through this event, God was teaching her to place her faith elsewhere, someplace more permanent and unshakable?

Read Genesis 12:17-20. How did God show up for her?

What does Genesis 12:17-20 reveal about God's nature? (His power, sovereignty, faithfulness, and ability to care for us?)

When has God revealed similar characteristics in your life? When has He shown Himself to be stronger than your fears and circumstances?

In what ways did that event or outcome strengthen your faith?

Pause to reflect on Psalm 46:1, which says, "God is our refuge and strength, a very present help in trouble" (ESV). Do you notice the emphasis this verse places on God's presence? The Creator of the universe isn't just present; He's very present, or present in abundance. Remember this as you go about your day and periodically pause to remind yourself that God is with you.

End your study time in prayer, asking God to help you recognize His constant presence and power.

Day Four
Forming Faith-Focused Neural Pathways
Read: Psalm 27

Chaos and terrifying situations can teach us to lean harder on Jesus, ultimately leading to freedom, or they can paralyze us. The outcome depends on our focus. I've shared briefly how, for years, I sought to control absolutely everything from my family life to our finances, out of fear. But then God intervened, allowed me to free-fall into a period of unemployment, so I could land securely in Him. And I did. When God stripped away many of the things I'd come to rely on, He helped me recognize, when everything else crumbled, He remained.

As a result, I walked out of that painful and frightening experience a little stronger, a little freer, and a great deal closer to Him. I believe this is exactly what happened with Sarah. God showed up for her in a huge and noticeable way. Scripture says He inflicted "serious diseases on Pharaoh and his household because of Abram's wife [Sarah]" (Gen. 12:17).

Think about that for a minute. That's the equivalent of God striking everyone in the White House with an illness—for you. Can you imagine the statement that must have made to Sarah? When she felt discarded, abandoned, and alone, God showed up.

Anchoring Ourselves in God

He does the same for us, and each time we encounter evidence of His power and grace, He's inviting us to know Him better. To trust Him more.

To replace our fear with faith.

Unfortunately, I haven't always responded this way. There've been times, like when a blur of fur bolted in front of me as I was cruising down the freeway, I allowed my fear of what could've happened to distract me from God's hand.

That morning, shortly after dropping my daughter off at school, I headed to St. Charles to conduct story research. The drive itself was pleasant, and I soon occupied myself with listening to the radio and plotting story elements in my head. About two hours out, a dog or coyote, I couldn't tell which, dashed in front of me out of nowhere. I must've been going 70 mph or more. The impact jolted me, but too shocked to react, I simply lifted my foot off the gas pedal and kept going. And beneath the shock and overriding it all, I felt a strange calm that largely stilled my reaction.

It took a while for my brain to catch up, prompted in part by a plume of smoke funneling up from my front end. Heart pounding, I slowly merged to the shoulder as cars continued to whiz by. I soon discovered my front end, including my radiator and fan, was smashed. I needed a tow truck to get home, which, at this point, was about two hours away. At a cost of about $3.50 per mile, that resulted in quite a bill!

Not to mention, my plans for the day were shot. And yet, as the man driving me back to Kansas City yapped away about all the accidents he'd seen over the years, I realized God had saved my life.

Though I-70 was relatively busy, I'd managed to have a pocket of space between myself and the cars behind me. But still, had I not been so shocked and instead chose to slam on my breaks, I likely would've triggered a multi-car pile up.

How Fears Grow

I praised God for my safety, but instead of taking time to meditate on His care, I soon focused on the fearful "what-ifs." Whenever I drove a long stretch of highway, I became hyper-alert, scanning the surrounding countryside for lingering animals. And while it's good to remain watchful, I took this to an extreme. My hands grew slick around the steering wheel and my muscles tightened. Drives I once used as private prayer and praise times focused on God became periods of self-obsession. As a result, instead of arriving at locations spiritually and emotionally refreshed, I showed up tense, irritable, and exhausted.

Somehow I'd trained my brain to become fearful when driving. I needed to redirect my thinking, or form new neural pathways, if you will.

After Abraham and Sarah's Egypt experience, I wonder which direction her thoughts took. As she lay on her mat each night, did she remind herself of her husband's betrayal, of the terror she felt, or the moment God intervened? Did she obsess over the sinfulness of man or meditate on the goodness of God? Did she replay her hurt or how God showed up in the middle of it?

In the Face of Danger

I love reading the Psalms, particularly those written by David, the Hebrew shepherd turned king. You may be familiar with his story. God anointed him Israel's ruler while a man named Saul still occupied the throne. Seeing God's hand on David, Saul became murderously jealous and spent the rest of his days hunting David down.

I don't know the size of Saul's army or the force behind him, but he was the reigning king and therefore someone to be feared! To put this in perspective, it'd be similar to having the president and his forces—CIA, FBI, military men—coming after you.

With his life threatened, David fled to the wilderness, hid in caves, and even pretended to be a madman in order to find refuge in a foreign land. But amidst all of his hardships and terror, he penned beautiful, desperate, and courage-invoking psalms reminding himself of God's power and calling his heart to faith.

Some believe he wrote Psalm 27 during this troubled period. Others think this passage arose later, when he was reviewing God's faithfulness throughout his life. Either way, David's words, preserved for us, can help bolster our hearts and insulate us from fear. If we're in a time of peace, we can train our minds to focus on truth before chaos hits—because it will. And if we're in the middle of uncertainty, we can avert our thoughts off our fears and follow David's example.

Read Psalm 27 and note words, phrases, or truths that stand out to you.

What does this passage reveal about God's heart?

How does this passage speak to you personally?

Review verse 1. What question did David repeat?

As if in answer, what three divine characteristics did David list?

What does verse 2 indicate about God and His power?

Read verses 3-6 and underline or make note of all David's "I will" statements.

Now read those verses again, making the same declarative statements.

Notice, David didn't say "I can" or "I should" be confident or seek out God's presence. It's almost as if he gave himself a pep talk or command.

When have you done something similar, when afraid or discouraged? What was the result?

If you were to write verse 3 according to your situation or fears, what would your "though" statements be?

What is David's one desire (v. 4)?

After discussing God's power against his fear, David says what he longs for most is to dwell in God's presence. Can you share a time when you were afraid or feeling unsettled and you pulled away to spend time with Jesus? What was the result?

Do you notice the conjunction in verse five? What does this conjunction connect?

In verse 5, what did David say God would do for him?

Do you sense David's desperation in verses 7-12?

According to verse 10, why did David long to learn God's ways?

When have you felt similar? Perhaps you were facing a significant health or financial challenge that left you confused. In what ways did your situation draw you to God and deepen your yearning for Him?

What is the tone of verse 13?

How can you speak hope into your current situation or perhaps a future difficulty?

What is David's tone in verse 14? Who is he talking to?

How often do you give yourself pep talks?

When afraid, are you more apt to paralyze yourself by focusing on your "enemies" or embolden yourself by focusing on God?

How might following David's example help you strengthen your faith muscles and develop new neural pathways?

Stop to think of situations during which you tend to become afraid. How can you direct your thoughts to truth during those moments?

End your study time in prayer, asking God to help you become more alert to your thought life and redirect negative thinking onto truth.

Day Five
A New Way of Thinking
Review: Genesis 12:10-20
Read: Proverbs 3:5-8, James 1:1-8

Have you worried yourself sick over something, only to have that *thing* later become a nonissue? Maybe that job loss you feared turned into a promotion, or an unexpected insurance reimbursement arrived in time to pay a bill.

For most of my life when uncertainties hit, I immediately developed a game plan—or ten. I strategized all the ways to avoid numerous potential messes—and believe me, my mind could fabricate plenty! Ultimately, I fell into self-reliance, acting like an orphan forced to face the big, ugly world alone. But nineteen times out of twenty, my most strategic and well-thought out plans not only ended in naught, but landed me in a mess. I've launched into hard discussions I never needed to have, applied for jobs God never intended for me, and wasted hours upon hours pestering my husband to follow along.

I've since learned that my wisdom, no matter how logical it seems, is faulty on my best day. My perspective is limited, and this is triply true when I'm anxious. My vision narrows onto my problem until I lose sight of everything else, including the fact that I have a Father who loves me and will never leave. He's big enough, powerful enough, and attentive enough to care for me.

He's big enough to care for you as well. I'm reminded of this truth whenever I read Sarah's story. I imagine fears plagued her from the moment she stepped outside of Ur. They must have turned to terror when the Pharaoh's men took her in. As she sat in his harem, likely with numerous other women, her thoughts must have spiraled. Her situation seemed hopeless. The one man she'd relied on had abandoned her. Who else could she turn to?

The God who called her, created her, loved her, and heard her desperate and even unspoken cries.

The same God who hears our every concern and wants to lead us to peace. A peace that extends far beyond our momentary circumstances. One that rests not on ever-shifting outcomes but instead on the unchanging Savior of the world.

So why do we waste so much time and energy entertaining fear when we could be focusing on truth instead?

Read Proverbs 3:5-8.

These verses may be familiar. If so, I encourage you to push past familiarity into ownership—determine to apply this passage with diligence. Prepare your mind today so you can face your next struggle or uncertainty with the confidence that comes from being firmly grounded in truth.

Pause to consider some of the things that make you anxious. What does it mean to trust the Lord in those situations? What might it look like for you to do so?

In what ways has God shown Himself trustworthy in your life?

Notice, in verse 5, Scripture tells us to trust in God with *all,* not part, of our hearts. Why do you believe the author of this passage added this emphasis?

What does partial trust look like?

Again, consider one of your anxieties. How do you tend to interpret that situation "according to your own understanding"?

When have you found your understanding of a situation to be faulty? Can you give a specific example?

How might "submitting" to God, as the NIV puts it, or "seeking God's will," as the NLT states, keep your path straight and your footing sure?

How does straying from God's path lead to danger?

Which behavior, submitting to God or straying from His will, ultimately produces the most fear and uncertainty?

Is there anything you need to do to align your life with God's will for you?

Sometimes obedience feels scary and involves risk, like when we fear it'll cost us our job or a relationship. But as I've often reminded myself, when facing an unpleasant decision, I'd rather receive God's blessings than His consequences. That blessing may be something financial, like when God honors integrity with a promotion, or it could be something even more precious like increased relational intimacy with Him and those He loves.

Courage Found in Love

When obedience feels challenging, how can remembering God's love help you obey with courage?

My fear meter rises considerably when chaos hits. I feel powerless against my circumstances and uncertain about which direction to take. When that happens, I take great comfort from James 1:1-8.

First, note whom James, the author, addresses in verse 1. He was writing to believers experiencing persecution and who likely battled fear daily. They didn't need to know how to prepare for possible trouble; they were in the midst of it! Christians were losing their homes, their employment, and their lives in the most brutal ways, and it appeared things would get worse.

They needed to know how to survive and stand strong when tyrants came pounding on their door. To which James responded, "Consider it all joy …"

I don't know about you, but that's the last thing I want to hear when trouble hits. That phrase is almost as irritating as my husband's admonitions to calm down when I feel afraid. But notice, James doesn't tell the ancient believers to rejoice in their circumstances. Instead, he encourages them to base their joy on God's grace and all He's doing in and through them.

In other words, to center and cement their thoughts on Christ and His love for them.

Easy to discuss, crazy-hard to do, especially when our fears are triggered. In those situations, most of us either lash out (fight) or shut down (flight). But James offers a better option in verse 5.

What is that?

How readily do you seek God's wisdom when you're afraid or experiencing challenging situations?

How might doing so help you grow in courage and confidence?

According to this passage, how does God respond when you ask Him for wisdom?

How does He expect us to respond once He gives that wisdom to us?

Have you been on a boat, kayak, or canoe on a windy day? I have, numerous times, and I'm always left seasick!

Tossed About

One summer, while vacationing in Hawaii, my daughter and I rented some paddleboats and ventured out into the ocean. While she quickly paddled off, I lay back on my board and allowed the current to carry me further and further from shore. Maybe thirty minutes later, I looked toward the beach and noticed with alarm how far I'd come. I quickly started to paddle back—only by this time, the waves had picked up. I paddled harder and harder without getting anywhere and toppled into the salty water again and again.

By the time I finally made it back, I was exhausted, my eyes stung, and my muscles felt numb and rubbery. (My daughter coasted in about an hour later looking as refreshed as she had when she first pushed out. Figures.)

Reading James's analogy of windblown waves reminded me of that salty, tiring, sunburned afternoon, one that took me much longer to get through than I'd initially anticipated. Staying atop my board would've been challenging enough. Add in some choppy water, and I soon wondered if I'd ever make it to shore.

The same often holds true in life. Our troubles, whether tragedy or fear or both combined, can cause even the strongest among us to grow weary. But the minute we start to doubt God's will and guidance, we land ourselves in a wind-churned tumult that thrashes us against the waves of uncertainty.

To stand strong we need to cast our anchors deep into God's unchanging nature and perfect wisdom. We do that by seeking His guidance and then determining to trust that what He says indeed is good and right and true.

Strength comes when we choose to trust that if we lean on Him, He will indeed carry us through whatever storm we're facing and gently deposit us safely on shore.

I don't know what Sarah was thinking when her husband betrayed her to the Pharaoh. I don't know what her prayers were like when she sat, waiting, in his harem. I don't know if she turned to God or felt abandoned by Him, but I do know how God responded. He saw her and rescued her—in love.

Scripture tells us God has no favorites and that He's loving to all His creation. Because of this, we know He's as committed to us as He was to Sarah. Nothing in all of creation can separate us from His love or pluck us from His hands.

As you close out this week, pause to commit your fears to God. If you're facing an uncertainty or difficult decision, ask for His guidance, then trust Him to lead you in His way and His perfect timing. Determine now to obey, whatever He asks, however He leads, knowing when you do, you'll be sinking your anchor down sure and deep.

Week Five: Waiting Well

Jennifer Slattery
Day 1, 2

Dena Dyer
Day 3, 4, 5

Week Five
Viewer & Group Discussion Guide
From the Video:

Notes from the video:

Group discussion Questions:
Note to leaders: You probably won't have time to get to all the questions. Please let the discussion guide you, and focus on those questions you feel most beneficial to your group members.

What resonated with you most during last week's lessons or Bible reading?

What resonated with you most during the video?

How well do you normally handle waiting?

When does waiting tend to be easier for you?

When is waiting most difficult for you?

When has God used a time of waiting to strengthen your faith?

Has God ever used a period of waiting to shift your priorities?

What does it mean to wait well?

What truths regarding God (His character, promises, or heart toward you) most help you to wait well?

Day One (Option One)
Understanding God's Story
Read: Genesis 13 and 14 or 15 (your choice) and Genesis 16:1-3
Note: If you have more time, read Genesis 13-16:3.

Who are the main characters in this passage?

What does this passage reveal about the human condition, such as:
- Mankind's rebellion against/obedience toward God?

- Mankind's attempts to fill their needs apart from Him or relying on Him for their needs?

- Mankind's attempts to reach Him on their own terms?

What does this passage reveal regarding God's nature?

What does this passage reveal about God's plans?

How might this passage reveal mankind's need for the gospel?

In what ways are you/have you been similar to one or more of the characters in this passage?

What might God want you to know through this section of Scripture?

What might He be asking you to do?

End your reading in prayer, asking God to help you apply His word and live out whatever you sense Him impressing on your heart.

Day One (Option Two)
Bible Study Application Tool: Commentaries
Read: Genesis 13 and 14 or 15 (your choice) and Genesis 16:1-3
Note: If you have more time, go ahead and read Genesis 13-16:3

Materials needed: Internet access

When I was first asked to write Bible study materials, I felt overwhelmed. No, *terrified* that I'd misunderstand, and therefore mis-teach, a portion of Scripture. Though I'd learned to be diligent when studying the Bible, I knew my propensity for error. And let's be honest; a lot of Scripture is vague and confusing.

For a while, this fear of getting things wrong paralyzed me and nearly kept me from obeying God's nudge. But then He reminded me that I didn't need to rely on my understanding alone. In fact, I wasn't supposed to. Back then, I had a senior editor who often resembled a Bible encyclopedia to rely upon. He was my "checks and balances" so to speak; the person to make certain my writing aligned with God's truth.

Accessing Bible Study Application Tools Online

Unfortunately, most of us won't be able to contact theologians when questions arise. But thanks to modern technology and God's provisionary grace, brilliant Bible scholars and their thoughts on Scripture are but a click away. This is a priceless blessing previous generations didn't have. Prior to the Internet and Bible study websites, if someone wanted to read Spurgeon's or Calvin's thoughts on a topic, they had to buy commentaries or visit a seminary library.

Today, we only have to navigate to a reputable Bible website to find answers to some of our most difficult questions and a well-educated filter for our thoughts or interpretations. You can find commentaries on Biblehub.com, the Blue Letter Bible, and Bible Study Tools. Simply type the name of your preferred site followed by the word "commentary" into your search engine browser. Then click on the relevant link that pulls up. This should lead you to that site's search engine. Here, type your verse or passage, then read the thoughts that follow.

Practice

How about we dig in using this week's reading as our practice text? Since we're focusing primarily on the long wait Sarah and Abraham experienced from the time they left Ur to when God blessed them with a child, let's look specifically at Genesis 15:1-21 and 16:1-3.

Always begin by first analyzing the text yourself.

What do you observe?

Who are the main characters in this passage?

What questions and thoughts does it initiate?

What words or phrases stand out to you?

What challenges, emotions, and thoughts would you have had at this point (or during this period) if you'd been Sarah?

Now find a relevant commentary or two.

Did they provide further insight or clarification?

End your reading in prayer, asking God to help you apply His word and live out whatever you sense Him impressing on your heart.

Day Two
Bible Study Application Tools: Historical/Cultural Context
Review: Genesis 13 and 14 or 15 (your choice) and Genesis 16:1-3
Note: If you have more time, go ahead and read Genesis 13-16:3

This week, we're covering a large span of time and thus a large amount of Scripture involving a great deal of historical and cultural context. Obviously, we won't have time to cover it all during the course of this study. Instead, we can allow our curiosity and the Holy Spirit to guide us. Since we're discussing the topic of waiting, I suggest you research one of the following:

Abraham and Lot separating (Genesis 13) and the issues involved—so that you can later draw inferences regarding Abraham's choice and what it showed regarding his faith, and God's response and what that showed regarding His faithfulness.

God's covenant with Abraham (Genesis 15) and any cultural customs related to Abraham's statement, or perhaps the importance of heirs in Bible times.

You can also research ancient covenants to discover the significance of the torch passing between the two carcasses in v. 17, or to understand the significance of God's covenant with Abraham.

What questions arise as you read that passage that could lead to further study? What verses or phrases indicate a potential cultural difference between Abraham's time and ours?

Journal your thoughts, questions, any interesting historical or cultural information you come across, and any additional thoughts or questions your research triggers. (To review/for a more in-depth guide, revisit the historical lesson from week one and two.)

End your study time in prayer, asking God to give you a hunger for Scripture and the perseverance to finish this study strong.

Day Three
God's Purposes in our Waiting
Review: Genesis 13-14
Read: Romans 8:24-30

While driving around town, I (Dena) have noticed a disturbing trend. If I take more than one second to hit the gas pedal after a light turns green, the driver behind me honks.

Maybe I'm getting slower, but I think the problem runs deeper. As a society, we are growing more impatient. Think about it: if our fast food doesn't come out fast enough, we complain. When an event or speaker goes long, we squirm and look at our phones. If our favorite show gets interrupted while we're streaming it, we groan. Technology has made our lives easier in some ways, but it has also made us feel entitled to have things instantly.

Or maybe that's just me.

During my forty-seven years of life, I've waited on more significant things, too. When I met my husband, I'd dated enough not-quite-right guys to realize Carey was the "one." But we remained in the "friend zone" for eleven long months before he realized I was the one for him. Later, as a young newlywed, I waited to conceive, then suffered an early miscarriage. I also waited and worked for five years, garnering fifty rejections, before becoming a published author.

God used each of these waiting seasons to teach me about Himself and reveal areas where He needed to work. He patiently and tenderly carved away my pride and self-sufficiency.

Sarah's Wait

Sarah knew impatience, too. In fact, she waited not for minutes or months but decades to see a promise fulfilled. God had told Abraham that He would make him into a great nation, with descendants too numerous to count. But He didn't reveal the "when" or the "how." In fact, until Genesis 17, Sarah wasn't mentioned at all, and she may have wondered how she fit with it all.

Most likely, the first few post-promise years were filled with hope and anticipation. As time sped by, though, and her body began to change and slow down, Sarah surely entertained doubts. Had Abraham heard God correctly? What if she or Abraham had done something to prevent the promise from being fulfilled? And most important—would the promised child have to come from her own womb?

Like many of us, Sarah saw an opportunity to "help God out" when she looked at her young slave, Hagar. She offered Hagar to her husband, justifying it in her humanness. Abraham, too, rationalized the action instead of seeking God's will on the matter.

I wonder if I'd have done the same.

From Confidence to Worry

Two years ago, my husband encouraged me to look for a steady job. At the time, I was a freelance writer and speaker, and I taught nine hours a week at my youngest's homeschool co-op. However, with our oldest son set to start college, we needed more income. Carey and I felt certain I was doing the right thing by resigning from the co-op.

As I began to search for jobs and update my resume, I prayed with confidence: "Lord, I know You have the right job for me. Please lead me to it. Thank You for Your provision for our family."

But as the weeks rolled on, my prayers felt stilted. The reaction to all the resumes I sent out? Crickets. I took a job teaching voice at a local children's theater academy a few hours a week, grateful for the income. And I connected with an editor who paid me to write short articles for a faith-based women's website. Still, our savings account balance dropped lower and lower, and I worried. I tried to figure out why hiring managers and HR folks continued to say, "Thanks but no thanks." Maybe I was too old, too out of touch with the job market, too *something*?

Old Patterns Creep Back In

As a teenager and young married woman, I often struggled with my identity in Christ. Due to childhood trauma, and because I coped through perfectionism, I had suffered depression, panic attacks, and anxiety. Thankfully, a series of godly counselors taught me to replace feelings of unworthiness with God's truth found in scripture.

But during my job search, I let myself slip into old, damaging patterns. At night, instead of sleeping peacefully and trusting God to provide (as He had countless times before), I attempted to figure out the problem for myself. Rather than seeking Him in prayer and reading the Bible, I sat at my computer and fretted at all hours. I compulsively searched and applied for any job within an hour's drive of our home that would use my talents at marketing, community relations, and writing. I preferred a non-profit or ministry job, but I widened the net to include editing, theater, and fundraising.

Like Sarah must have, I felt perfectly fine about helping God out. In my sinful state of doubt and impatience, I chose to ignore the fact that the phrase "God helps those who helps themselves" doesn't appear in the Bible.

Suddenly, a job appeared which seemed perfect. The director of the theater academy where I taught voice resigned unexpectedly, and I applied for the position. The search committee immediately asked me to come in for an interview, and later, my friend who sat on the board told me I had "dazzled" the team.

However, a second interview led not to a job offer, but a phone call from my friend. "I am so, so sorry," he said. "It was a terribly difficult decision. We had four meetings in two days and ultimately, the committee decided to go with the other applicant." Stunned, I hung up and dissolved in tears.

Is Waiting Time Wasted Time?

I pouted for a few days after that rejection. My sweet husband consoled me, but then kindly jolted me with a simple statement: "Dena, you're not resting in God."

Trusting

Ouch. As much as it pained me, I had to admit Carey was right. In humility and sorrow, I repented of my drivenness and impatience. I asked God to forgive me and strengthen me in this difficult season of waiting. Most importantly, I resolved to pray before applying for other jobs.

As I prayed, I distinctly felt the Holy Spirit say, "Don't waste the waiting." I understood this to mean that I was to submit and trust, instead of running ahead of my Heavenly Father.

Five more months passed before I saw an ad for a job that was an even better fit than the offer I'd narrowly missed. A few days later, after a whirlwind of applying and interviewing, I had the job. I'm still there; in fact, I've been promoted and received a raise. It's my favorite job, ever.

Read Romans 8:24-30.

What does Paul, the author, say to the Roman church in this passage about God's purposes for us as His children?

How does the Holy Spirit help us as we wait for God's promise(s) to be fulfilled?
What part does hope play in our waiting?

Think back to what we've been learning about Sarah. What did she hope for?

Journal about a time you ran ahead of God and any consequences (physical, mental, emotional, and/or spiritual) you experienced afterwards.

If you're currently in a waiting mode, what might God want to teach you during this season?

Have you ever "wasted the waiting"? Explain.
What did you learn from that painful time?

What do you think it means to be called according to God's purpose?

Considering this, what purpose might our waiting serve?

End your study time in prayer, asking God to center you in His love for you and to help you trust His timing as He seeks to make you more like Christ.

Day Four
What We Can't See
Review: Genesis 16.
Read: 2 Peter 3:8-9; Exodus 14:14.

When we were in our early forties, my husband and I went through a devastating season of disappointment. A position we had moved our young family for didn't work out as we'd hoped. We felt we had no choice but to move again and start over in a different town, closer to my family. I found a full-time job I loved, but Carey was stuck substitute teaching and working part-time at a local yogurt shop. He hated our new town, didn't like our apartment, and felt like a failure because he wasn't the primary breadwinner. His resulting depression broke my heart and created a huge gulf between us. In short, he was miserable, and he let me know it.

I prayed for him, cried buckets of frustration over our situation, and questioned God: Why hadn't the job we'd felt Him leading us to accept three years earlier worked out? I tried to get Carey to go to counseling with me, but he refused. Looking back, I can see he was having a mid-life crisis and didn't know how to ask for help.

Running Ahead—Again

About a year into our move, I came up with what I thought was a great idea: I'd look for a house to buy. A friend assured me we could get a loan with a decent interest rate. We didn't want to make our two sons change schools again, so I felt confident that we'd remain in town long enough for our oldest (who was 12 at the time), to graduate high school. Surely that would financially justify buying a home. After all, we wouldn't be throwing our money down a rent hole, and being out of our cramped—though clean and pretty--apartment would cheer Carey up.

Unfortunately, I neglected to pray about any of that. Instead, I forged ahead and made my own plans. Carey agreed, we got approved for a mortgage, looked at houses, and purchased one in a neighborhood close to the boys' Christian school.

We didn't realize God was working behind the scenes on a job offer for Carey at a church he'd worked at previously. Not two months after we made the first house payment, he got a call from the head of the search committee in a community we adored and where we (and the boys) had tons of friends.

At first, he told them he wasn't interested, because we didn't want to relocate again. However, through prayer, we realized God did want Carey to accept the position. It would use all his talents and provide for our family in numerous ways. The boys were excited about moving to a place they'd once loved, and we were thrilled that we'd all have a built-in support system. The church even wanted to pay for our moving expenses.

The downside: we were forced to rent out the house we'd bought, long distance, for three years before it sold (and we broke even). God protected us, because we could have lost many thousands of dollars by running ahead of Him. Instead of trying to make my husband happy and engineer circumstances to everyone's benefit, I should've asked God for wisdom and discernment. I learned a lot from my failure to rest, pray—and wait.

What Sarah Couldn't See

So I really "get" Sarah. I understand how she might have wanted to make Abraham happy and provide an heir through Hagar. After all, that sort of thing was an accepted practice in biblical times.

Sarah wasn't aware of how God was working behind the scenes. She only saw what was on the surface: She was too old to bear children. Abram was old, as well. Hagar was a slave of child-bearing age.

Hagar did conceive, and when she did, she treated Sarah with contempt. In response, Sarah mistreated Hagar, and then Hagar ran away. God called her back, told her to submit to her imperfect mistress, and a few months later, Hagar bore Abram a son named Ishmael.

However, Ishmael was not the "child of promise."

Our impulsive actions—even those done with good intentions—can harm us and others. That's why we must be prayerful, penitent, and patient. We see the surface of things, but God sees all. We must trust Him to work out His plans in His way and time.

Ponder this quote, from leadership expert John Maxwell:

> "Joseph waited fourteen years in prison for a crime he didn't commit. Noah waited 120 years for the predicted rains to arrive. Job waited perhaps a lifetime, 60-70 years, for justice. God prepares leaders in a slow cooker, not in a microwave oven…waiting deepens and matures us, levels our perspective, and broadens our understanding. Tests of time determine whether we can endure seasons of seemingly unfruitful preparations and indicate whether we can recognize and seize the opportunities that come our way.[6]"

Read 2 Peter 3:8-9. Spend some time prayerfully considering these verses.

What does this passage say about the nature of time in God's economy?

Do you often see time from God's perspective, or are you mostly concerned with your day-to-day troubles? (Be honest!) Explain.

In Matthew Henry's commentary on this passage, he says, "What men count slackness, is long-suffering … it is giving more time to His own people, to advance in knowledge and holiness, and in

---

[6] https://bit.ly/2PVMNdu

the exercise of faith and patience, to abound in good works, doing and suffering what they are called to, that they may bring glory to God.[7]"

Read Exodus 14:14.

Think about a time (or times) when you decided to act, instead of waiting on God in prayer and stillness. What happened? Would you do something different if you could go back and change the past?

Journal about what God might be doing as He allows you to wait. How might He use your waiting time to advance your knowledge and holiness?

End your study in prayer. Ask God to forgive you for the times you've run ahead of Him. Thank Him for the biblical wisdom He gives through His word and the stories of those people, like Sarah, who became pillars of the faith (even though they were oh-so-human!). Ask Him for the discipline to be still and rest in Him, knowing that He has a divine plan, one which includes your spiritual growth.

---

[7] https://bit.ly/2PVMNdu

Day Five
Surrendering to God's Plan
Review: Genesis 16.
Read: 2 Corinthians 4:1, 7-12, 16-18.

The other night, I had a terrible dream. In it, my husband Carey became intimate with another woman—with my permission! But after he had slept with the mystery girl, I became murderously angry and deeply depressed.

Though the nightmare felt vividly real, when I woke up, I realized my subconscious had combined Carey's recent busy work schedule with my study of Sarah and Hagar. And now, I more deeply comprehend how Sarah might have felt. I can understand how viciously she might have mistreated Hagar and how Hagar perhaps feared for her life enough to flee to the desert alone.

Sexual intimacy connects men and women to their spouses on a spiritual and emotional, not just a physical, level. It also helps them focus on their loved one in a carnal culture. Plus, it can help keep them from becoming envious of another person's influence over their mate or jealous of their spouse's attentions.

Since God created us, He knows our weaknesses. He sees our secret thoughts, darkest fears, and shameful acts. And as Max Lucado says, "He loves us as we are but cares too much to leave us that way" (paraphrased).

If we surrender to God's plan during a season of intense and/or prolonged waiting, He can mold our character and teach us spiritual lessons. Later, He'll use those truths and our deepened growth as we serve Him.

However, the reverse is true as well. When we don't surrender to God, we're left vulnerable to all sorts of temptations.

Big Dreams, Deferred

I've longed to sing professionally since childhood. I ate, slept, and breathed music. My parents encouraged my talent, and even though I lived in a little town in Texas with limited opportunities, God placed teachers and mentors in my path to help me. By my sophomore year in high school, I'd made All-State choir and starred in several local productions.

However, after graduation, I transitioned from my small burg to the Baylor University music school. There, almost every time I auditioned for a solo, production, or group, I was named an alternate or understudy.

I began to doubt my abilities and wondered if I had a future in music. I also struggled with envy. I looked at the other girls who were chosen for parts and thought, *I wish it were me. Why can't it be me?!*

Like Sarah, I longed for the fulfillment of a dream, and I struggled with deferred hope.

For nearly three years, I felt out of place and continued to wrestle with jealousy, frustration, and a lack of confidence. It wasn't until my senior year that I had the courage to audition for a music theater group I had long admired. No surprise: I was chosen as an alternate soprano. However, that summer a group member decided to transfer to another school, and I moved up into her spot.

The year I spent in Baylor Showtime was full of a demanding rehearsal schedule, buckets of sweat--and loads of fun. And as it happened, the professor over the group recommended me for a post-graduate touring group, in which I met my husband.

Looking back, I wished I'd auditioned sooner. Who knows if I could have been involved with Showtime for two or three years instead of one? Perhaps I missed out because I forgot who I was in Christ—beloved, chosen, gifted, and special—and instead fed my insecurities and doubts.

God taught me an important lesson from that experience. Jealousy and envy hurt me most. Also, years on the bench made me more grateful when opportunities came my way.

When God fulfilled her dream of motherhood, I think Sarah felt more grateful than those women whose fertility blossomed early and often. Because she knew how desolate empty arms felt, she celebrated when they were full.

Sinful Tendencies

In my mid-twenties, a similar set of circumstances showed me that God still had much work to do in my heart. In the spring after we married, Carey and I auditioned for a professional Christian musical production on the life of Christ—one I had seen and thought about participating in for some time. The director spoke so highly of both Carey and me that after we sang, we felt confident he'd offer us roles.

Carey was cast in a leading part—but I was chosen for the large chorus and as an understudy for one of the leading ladies.

Understudy again? I thought. *I am so tired of this!* Though I'm ashamed to admit it now, I became jealous of Carey. I was also envious of the woman cast in the role I had to learn but not perform.

Sinful much? Sigh. Even though I'd been a Christian since I was seven years old, I still had a long way to go in order to be Christlike. I questioned my appearance, talent, and personality. And I felt sorry for myself. Always the bridesmaid, never the bride …

It's clear now: God wanted more for me than applause and accolades. Throughout my teens and twenties, I set loftier and loftier goals for myself and was never satisfied. Instead of working on things I could control—by reading the Bible, honing my talents, and praying for God to use me as He thought best—I worked against myself. By focusing on accomplishments rather than obedience, I robbed myself of contentment.

Thankfully, God broke me of my perfectionism a few years later. It wasn't fun, and it didn't happen overnight. But I'm unspeakably grateful that He didn't give up on me.

He didn't give up on Sarah, either. In Genesis 17, when she overheard that God's promise would include her and laughed, He could have said, "That's it! I can't work with her. I'll use Hagar to fulfill the covenant I made with Abraham." But He didn't. He stuck with His plan.

Friend, do you know what this means? God won't give up on you.

Our Heavenly Father is so immeasurably good to us. While we wait—often with impatience or envy—He waits with us. Like a master craftsman, He hones and perfects our rough edges. He loves us too much to leave us as we are. His goal is to make us more like Jesus, and He is a patient, loving artist. He sees the women we were created to be and isn't content until we're fully transformed into those people.

Take comfort in these truths as you endure your own waiting season.

Read 2 Corinthians 4:1 and 4:7-12.

Think about a ministry God has called you to, whether to your family or the wider world. What circumstance can cause you to lose heart, and what might God want to say to you through this passage?

Regarding verses 7-9, the IVP New Testament Commentary states, "The marvel of Paul's statement is not to be overlooked. The Christian … is a vessel made of common, run-of-the-mill clay—fragile and easily broken, and yet God has entrusted the treasure of the gospel to such a vessel, just as Palestinians stored their valuables in common clay pots. Why does God do this? According to Paul, He does it to show that this all-surpassing power is from God and not from us. God uses what is fragile and yet serviceable so that there might be no mistaking the origin of the gospel minister's power.[8]"

Ponder where you feel broken or fragile. Ask God to give you strength and endurance, and help you trust His plan, purposes, and timing.

The Greek word translated "power" is *dynamis*, from which we get the English "dynamite." God's abilities and understanding far exceed ours. Often, He allows us to remain in seemingly-impossible situations so that He gets the glory when the circumstance is ultimately resolved.

Read 2 Corinthians 4:16-18.

Why do you think Paul, the author, repeated the phrase, "we do not lose heart"?

---

[8] https://www.biblegateway.com/passage/?search=2+corinthians+4&version=NIV

Jot down a few thoughts about how you might fix your eyes on God and things of eternal value rather than temporary concerns. Then pen a prayer to God about who He is--and who you are--in light of His character, power, and mercy.

Week Six:
Moving Past Self-Sufficiency

Jennifer Slattery

Order of completion:

<u>Large Group time:</u>

- Discuss the previous week's lessons on pages 83-97 and share anything that resonated with you or surprised you in the reading.

- Watch Becoming His Princess Week Two: Unshakable Security Video found on the Wholly Loved Ministries' YouTube channel (Search YouTube + Wholly Loved).

- Discuss the video as a group using the discussion questions on page 102.

<u>Home lessons:</u>

- Day one: Choose one of the 2 options provided (p. 103 and 104).

Complete the remaining week's lessons as provided.

Week Six:
Viewer & Group Discussion Guide
From the Video:

When we allow fear, pride, or desperation to drive our actions, we step further from _____ _____ and choose our _____, and _____ over His.

_____ and _____ are closely intertwined.

We experience the life Christ died to give us, in all its fullness, through _____.

Pride and self-sufficiency blind us to God's _____ and _____.

God gave us the Old Testament commands and requirements to bring us to the end _____ _____ that we'd find _____ _____.

When we strive for control, we trade our _____ in Christ for _____ and _____.

God offers us a two-part invitation: _____ to Him to find rest and to _____ from Him.

We learn from God when we _____ His voice. We find rest when we _____ to what we hear.

We find our greatest strength through _____.

In Matthew 11:29, Jesus said, _____
_____

Group Discussion Questions:

Note to leaders: You probably won't have time to get to all the questions. Please let the discussion guide you, and focus on those questions you feel most beneficial to your group members.

What resonated with you most from last week's lessons or Bible reading?

What resonated with you most from the video?

When have you seen fear lead to someone grasping or striving for control? What was the result?

During her video, Jennifer asked what it might take for you to tell your spouse to sleep with another woman. Is there any situation in which you would do that?

How does striving for control distance you from God's presence, plans, and power?

Jennifer suggested fear and self-sufficiency are intertwined. Do you agree or disagree, and why?

Do you feel it is easier for you to trust Christ for your salvation than it is in your day-to-day struggles? If so, why do you think that is?

When do you most tend to rely on yourself (choose self-sufficiency over surrender)? Why do you think this is?

In what ways does self-sufficiency blind us to God's presence and hand?

How does surrender lead to freedom and fullness of life?

Day One (Option One)
Understanding God's Story
Read: Genesis 16 & 21:1-21

Who are the main characters in this passage?

What does this passage reveal about the human condition, such as:
- Mankind's rebellion against/obedience toward God?

- Mankind's attempts to fill their needs apart from Him or relying on Him for their needs?

- Mankind's attempts to reach Him on their own terms?

What does this passage reveal regarding God's nature?

What does this passage reveal about God's plans?

How might this passage reveal mankind's need for the gospel?

In what ways are you/have you been similar to one or more of the characters in this passage?

What might God want you to know through this section of Scripture?

What might He be asking you to do?

End your reading in prayer, asking God to help you apply His word and live out whatever you sense Him impressing on your heart.

Day One (Option Two)
Bible Study Application Tool: Topical and Word Studies
Review: Genesis 16 & 21:1-21

We've already noted the importance of paying attention to repeated words and phrases in Scripture. When you read the Bible as one cohesive work pointing to an ultimate truth, Jesus, you will notice repeated themes. This is especially true in the book of Judges, where each segment of history reveals the gospel: God's people rebel and turn to foreign gods, they reap the consequences of their sin and are conquered by a warring nation, they repent and cry out to God for mercy, and He sends someone (a foreshadowing to Jesus) to save them. Once delivered, life goes well for a while, but they soon turn to sin and the cycle is repeated.

We see a rather intriguing element, soon to be repeated, in Sarah's story as well. God begins by telling us she's barren. From her culture's standpoint, this was her most defining characteristic, but in chapter 17 we see it also points to her greatest miracle—her grace story—when God gave her and Abraham a child and did for her what she couldn't do for herself.

God's Hand Revealed

If you were to continue through the Old Testament, you would notice God often used barren women to further His plans and save His people. In fact, many prominent Bible characters, including our Savior, were born to women who were either unable to have children or, in the case of Jesus' mother, had no means at the time to do so.

Consider:
- Sarah, who gave birth to Isaac, the child of promise (Genesis 11:27-21).
- Rebekah, who gave birth to Jacob, the father of the twelve tribes of Israel (Genesis 25:19-26).
- Rachel, who gave birth to Joseph, the Hebrew turned slave-turned-second in command (and who, like the "saviors" in the book of Judges, is a "type" or picture of Christ) (Genesis 29:31-30:22).
- The unnamed woman who birthed Samson, the strong warrior who freed God's people from the Philistines during the time of Judges (Judges 13, 15).
- In the New Testament, Elizabeth, the mother of John the Baptist, the prophet who prepared the way for Jesus (Luke 1:5-25, 57-80).

When you have more time, you may want to read and compare each of those and other similar accounts.

Biblical Examples

One way to find similar themes, like the one listed above, is to go to BibleHub.com and type "barrenness" into the site's search engine. When you do, a dropdown list of options will appear. One of these will say: "barrenness (topical)." Click on that.

A page will pull up with a paragraph from a Bible Dictionary (similar to an encyclopedia), a basic definition, and various related reference verses. Find the definition that fits what you're looking for. Here you'll find verses listed where that word appears. Click on this and flip back in your Bible to find where that particular story begins. As you read each account, make a list of things you note and questions you have. Look for similarities and differences between the various accounts.

What do they tell you about God?

How does each story reveal God's nature, an element of His promises, or His plan?

In what ways does that narrative reveal or point to the gospel?

Another intriguing "topical" element you may enjoy studying is revealed in Genesis 21:17—the Angel of the Lord. Many scholars believe this reference has special meaning. To discover what and why, follow the same steps as outlined above, make note of various places the Angel of the Lord is mentioned, read the story surrounding those verses, and make comparative notes on each.

Word Studies

Conducting word studies provides another way for us to deepen our understanding of certain elements of Scripture. Using today's passage as an example, you might choose to study the word "circumcised" (Gen. 16:10). You might find it fascinating to see how God carries this idea into the New Testament and how it relates to grace!

Word and topic studies can take a great deal of time, which you likely don't have now. When you're finished with *Becoming His Princess*, however, you may choose to return to this lesson to deepen your understanding of a word, phrase, or repeated theme and how it relates to God's story of redemption.

For now, considering what you've read today, why do you think Sarah's barrenness was significant?

In what ways does her barrenness point to the gospel?

End your reading in prayer, asking God to help you apply His Word and live out whatever you sense Him impressing on your heart.

Day Two
Historical/Cultural Context
Review: Genesis 16:1-15

We've discussed how easy it is to read 21st century culture into biblical text, leading to misunderstandings and false assumptions. We can do the same with God's commands, interpreting His directives through societal norms without realizing we're doing this. If we're not careful, our current customs and viewpoints can drastically hinder our understanding of God, His ways, and His plans.

Consider Genesis 16. Upon first reading this passage, most of us probably recoil. It's hard to understand how someone could ever encourage her husband to sleep with another woman! Then for him to go along with this, seemingly without even the slightest objection? Then put yourself in poor Hagar's position, a woman ripped from her homeland, forced into slavery, and now, another man's bed, one likely much older than her.

How could Sarah and Abraham, God's "called" couple, ever treat another human in such a way?

Understanding Cultural Influences

I may never truly understand the heart behind their actions, but my disgust and indignation is tempered, ever so slightly, once I understand the cultural elements surrounding this event. Before I share more, take a moment to consider how culture might have impacted Sarah and Abraham's actions.

In what ways is modern culture different?

How would this story change if you were to rewrite it to fit today's culture? Thinking this way, or even taking time to rewrite the narrative, can help us become alert to cultural differences that in turn can direct our research.

Seen By God

One thing's clear—women have not always been treated well! We discussed this in part early in our study when considering Sarah's label of barrenness. Today, we'll look at what it may have been like to be a female *and* a slave in ancient times. When we understand how little value Hagar likely held in the eyes of others—that it was completely reasonable, to their way of thinking, for Abraham to make her his sex slave—God's interaction with her becomes all the more beautiful! God saw her, spoke to her, and assured her that, despite her pain and mistreatment, everything was going to be okay.

That encounter must've completely blown her mind. Whether she was born into slavery, sold off by poor parents, or landed in servitude after some other misfortune, Hagar spent most of her life living without rights or any expectation of them. Considered property, she could be purchased, gifted, sold, and exploited. She lived to make other's lives easier and, in this instance, to provide what her mistress could not—a child.

As cruel and depraved as it may seem, laws allowed the powerful and wealthy to use their slaves as surrogates, as happened with Hagar. When pregnancy occurred, the child became the property of the slave owner. In this way, Sarah could claim she'd given Abraham a firstborn son and heir.

Hagar's Plight

So, not only was Hagar forced to relinquish the most sacred parts of herself, but she could also be forced to give up her most treasured possession.

As a mom who fell in love with her baby the moment I knew I'd conceived, I can't imagine the heartache, anger, hopelessness, and bitterness that must've invaded Hagar's heart. Her only consolation, if indeed she had any, was the fact that Abraham welcomed her not into his haram but instead into his "home" as a second wife.

As if polygamy was any better.

However, to Sarah and Abraham's way of thinking, this made perfect sense. That was how people did things, how families were built, land passed down, and names were continued.

But through a series of events that followed, God revealed to all of them that this wasn't His way. And so, continuing the worldview shift He began when He first called Abraham and Sarah out of Ur, God showed them just how contrary human ideals, practices, and wisdom often are to His.

God's Hand

In every encounter, difficult circumstance, and faith-filled reaction, God is molding us into the courageous, peace-filled women He created us to be. As we allow God to transform our thinking, He reveals those lies we believe and those false identities and ideals we cling to, so that we can find ourselves in Him.

So that His truth, and nothing but His truth, becomes ours.

And Sarah and Abraham for sure needed some major worldview shifting!

As do we.

Day Three
Uncovering the Root of Self-Reliance
Review: Genesis 16:1-3
Read: Genesis 3:1-6, 13, 16-24

Self-reliance and surrender are mutually exclusive, though both are birthed in love. It's the object of our affections that makes all the difference. Self-love, which inevitably fuels self-reliance, destroys people and relationships and can throw us completely off God's plan for us.

When we love Christ first and foremost, however, everything else shifts back into alignment.

Some portions of Scripture inspire me to live and behave better; other sections help me release a long, slightly dramatic sigh of relief. I like knowing I'm not the only one who makes mistakes and acts like an idiot on occasion. I've done a lot of crazy, stupid, self-deceived things in my day, but I've yet to force another woman on my man, or to force my man onto another woman.

In Genesis 16, Sarah did both. Somewhere between the moment of her betrayal and terror in Egypt to this point in the narrative, she became the oppressor—the one who used someone else as a commodity in order to get what she wanted.

When Desire Controls Behavior

Unmet desire, and the idolatry that often follows, can do that to a person. And though most of us have never trafficked a subordinate, as Sarah did Hagar, I'm fairly certain we've all manipulated and connived to get what we wanted.

The results are never pretty. People get hurt, trust shatters, and relationships take a heavy, sometimes irreparable hit.

Whenever we seek to meet our needs and find fulfillment apart from Christ, ugliness follows.

As a leader, I'm constantly fighting against pride and learning to live in the tension between spurring my team to excellence and offering grace. I don't always know where the line lies between those two Christ-centered realities, but there's one guaranteed way to override both: through self-obsession, also known as self-love.

The Power of Surrender

We overcome both through surrender. This goes much deeper than simply saying we don't have the ability to get from A to B. Surrender isn't simply relinquishing the oomph behind our steps but involves the willingness to abandon those steps all together. It's having the courage and heart to say, "Lord, even if You take this from me, even if You lead me in a direction I don't want to go, I still choose to yield to You."

It's intentionally returning to our first steps of faith—that day when we first heard the call to follow. When we chose Jesus over all else, knowing we'd find everything we need in Him.

Knowing apart from Him, we couldn't survive, not today nor in eternity.

Until we align our hearts with God's and His mission, we'll forever be grasping, striving, and conniving, as Sarah and Abraham did in today's passage. Granted, as we discussed yesterday, they likely thought their actions were acceptable. Why remain childless when one had a perfectly healthy, young slave who could bear children in your stead?

Confusion and Doubt

After a decade of infertility, they may even have wondered if they'd misunderstood God's promises. What if Abraham's descendants were never meant to come through Sarah? Considering how others viewed women at the time, and how Sarah likely thus viewed herself, she may have assumed God's promise to Abraham wasn't meant for her at all.

By this point, Sarah seemed to have grown completely exasperated with her own inadequacy and her husband's guidance. After all, look where that had landed her! She followed his lead, trusted his claims of divine revelation, left her homeland, only to find herself smack in the center of a famine. Then, her husband got a brilliant idea to travel to Egypt, with its plentiful crops and fattened livestock, only to toss her into the center of a haram! Then, just when things begin to settle down, this man who was supposed to protect and provide for her, gave up the best portion of his land for his nephew Lot, who'd been traveling with them.

And through each upheaval, difficulty, and betrayal, she'd remained the dutiful, submissive wife. But not anymore. It was time she stood up and solved her problems herself. As the old adage says, "If you want something done right …"

But notice, she wasn't only frustrated with her husband. According to Genesis 16:2, who did she ultimately blame for her condition?

What tone can you sense in her words?

Does her statement reveal a surrendered heart or a defiant one?

What might a surrendered heart look like in this situation?

What does her statement here reveal regarding how she viewed God's character?

It's as if she's saying, "God's holding out on me." Such thinking breeds countless other grace-distancing thoughts, like: *He must not care how I feel. He doesn't truly love me. God loves*—insert the names of whoever has what she doesn't but longs for—*more than me.*

All these defeating, misery-and-sin-producing conclusions arose from one falsehood: God's holding out on me.

This lie has been wreaking havoc with women's joy and peace from the beginning of time. In fact, it was at the root of the fall of man.

Read Genesis 3:1-6.

What did Eve believe God was keeping from her?

List some characteristics you know to be true about God.

How might remembering those truths about God have kept Eve from sinning?

When have you felt as if God was holding out on you in some way?

How might remembering His love, righteousness, faithfulness, and goodness have helped counter your negative thinking?

A while back, my writing career seemed to hit a dead end, one that left me frustrated, discouraged, and confused. It felt as if God had led me in a certain direction, had stirred my heart toward something, only to take that thing from me. For a while, my prayers took on an entitled, whiny tone. My attitude resembled Sarah's in Genesis 16:3. But then the words from Psalm 17:5, which I'd memorized previously, came to mind, inviting me to focus on what I knew to be true.

This verse says, "Great is our Lord, and abundant in power; His understanding is beyond measure" (ESV).

Belief Revealed

I realized I either believed God was all-powerful, loving, and wise, or I didn't. Yet, if I truly believed He not only knew the best course of action for every situation, but always and only did what was for my very best, then I had no reason to feel discouraged. Nor did I have any reason to strive, grasp, or connive.

Instead, I could spend my time and energy drawing closer to Him, learning to know His will, and trusting Him to bring it about in His way, timing, and according to His plan.

Which is always so much better than mine!

In fact, whenever I fail to seek God's will and instead follow my own, I almost always land in a mess, like Sarah did. Our tendency to botch things up through self-reliance isn't new. We humans have been behaving this way since the beginning of time.

The Danger of Self-Reliance

Read Genesis 3:16-24. What did Eve's rebellion and self-reliance (trying to fill her desires in her own strength and wisdom) cost her?

By grasping for what she didn't have, she lost most of what she did, and she found that which she gained—knowledge of good and evil—wasn't what she'd hoped it would be. You see, prior to that moment, she had full knowledge of good; everything she experienced to that point was nothing but good and right and pure and … amazing. Plus, she already had an intellectual knowledge of sin (evil) when God commanded her and Adam not to disobey Him. When she rebelled, however, her eyes were indeed opened and she knew, through experience, what sin felt like. Worse, that first sin opened the door for a host of other evils—violence, hatred, fear, sickness, death.

That was a knowledge God knew she could live her whole life without. But unconvinced of His goodness, she chose self-reliance over surrender and in so doing stepped out from under His protection.

Our world has suffered the consequences ever since.

Aligned With God

But I can't judge her too harshly, because there've been many times I've acted much the same. I suspect you have as well. We're a rebellious, short-sighted, self-reliant bunch and likely will always fight against our wayward wills this side of heaven. But when temptation hits, may we pause to ask ourselves: Is there anything worth stepping out from under the blessings and protection of the God who loves us?

And on that note, I encourage you to end this lesson in prayer, forsaking your wisdom and ways for God's, asking Him to give you the strength and the courage to wait on and trust in Him. To rely on Him—His guidance and plan—rather than yourself.

Day Four
In Need of Rescue
Read: Genesis 16:4-15

Brianna[9] wasn't exactly sure how it happened. One minute, she was at a party, laughing and drinking, flirting and playing coy. The next, she found herself in the back of a car, being groped by hands that pulled and tugged … and took. She couldn't call it rape. She'd entered the vehicle willingly, and really, she hadn't resisted. She hadn't said anything—no words of consent or refusal. She simply accepted.

She never said no. Though she'd wanted to. The entire time, she'd wanted to, and yet, she remained silent. "It's too late," she thought. Too late in the moment and too late in life. Though she didn't realize it at the time, she hadn't just relinquished her body. She'd given up on herself.

Somehow, somewhere, she'd lost her voice. If you'd asked her when or how, she couldn't tell you. All she knew was in that moment that will forever be cemented in her mind, she felt … worthless. It wasn't so much that she didn't have power to rise up and protect herself. Rather, she decided she wasn't worth the fight.

Losing self

That night began a self-degrading cycle of backseats, bedrooms, and hotel rooms as she drifted further and further from grace. She longed for God's love, for Him to reach into her mess and pluck her out, but she felt too far gone.

And so, to guard her heart from shattering beyond repair, she began to erect walls. To self-protect by hardening herself against the slightest vulnerability. Then no one could hurt her or let her down. Nor could they use and discard her if she was the one to willingly, emotionlessly, give herself away. And so, she began to leverage the very thing she lost. She'd use her sexuality to her advantage.

She didn't need a rescuer. Through determination and resolve, she would save herself—from pain, from need and rejection.

Never again would she feel so defenseless and exposed.

The Danger of Self-Protection

But this came at a cost. In guarding her heart against pain, she simultaneously closed herself off to freedom, healing, and love. She needed Someone stronger, bigger—gentle and patient—to break through her barricade of fear.

---

[9] Name changed for privacy purposes

Perhaps you've been there. Maybe you know the hurt of being used and discarded, of paying the consequences of someone else's sin. You know what it's like to feel powerless. And maybe, having climbed out of your moment of pain, you refuse to feel vulnerable ever again. In your determination to avoid pain or rejection, you've learned to rely on yourself. If you never form close relationships, if you never let anyone in, if you're completely self-sufficient physically, mentally, and emotionally, then you'll never again find yourself in a place of such need.

So long as you never depend on another, no one can let you down or hurt you.

But then you found yourself thrust into loneliness. You haven't avoided pain. You've simply swapped one kind—the kind caused by others—for that which is self-imposed.

Self-reliance leads to bondage, but Christ died to set us free. Freedom not from painful circumstances but instead from their power over us.

Do you want that? Does your heart cry out to be loved, to be healed, to experience a joy and peace that prevails over the darkest moments and encounters?

Trapped

I wonder how Hagar felt, as she moved from slave, to surrogate, to wife. How did she feel when her body was offered to another? Though she'd lost her voice the moment she became a slave, she lost her dignity, and likely a piece of her heart, once Abraham forced her into his bed.

Was that Hagar's first time? Or was she used to being consumed? To feeling powerless and insignificant?

Perhaps she saw this act, this giving of herself, as a step up—a necessary price to pay to earn her freedom. Though she still technically belonged to her mistress, her status shifted from Hagar the slave to Abraham's second wife and the mother of his child. Remember, in the ancient world, barrenness was viewed as a curse and fertility as divine favor.

Here we see Hagar's dishonor being lifted while Sarah's remained.

According to Genesis 16:4, how did Hagar respond to this turn of events?

How did Sarah respond to Hagar in verse 5?

Who does Sarah blame for the mess she created?

We often do that, don't we? Tumble headfirst into a thorn patch. Then blame others for our pricks instead of owning up to our sins and mistakes and asking God for mercy? The result—more brokenness and pain.

Now Abraham was caught between two wives, one of whom teetered between her position of spouse and slave. Ultimately, her slavery won out, and Abraham encouraged Sarah to "do as she will." She apparently did, and Hagar ran away (v. 6).

How do you think Hagar felt at this point?

Who, humanly speaking, did she have to rely on?

First she'd been torn from her homeland. Then, rejected by her mistress and spouse, she takes off into the wilderness. While pregnant.

Without a shelter or convenience store or food bank in sight. I have no idea how she hoped to survive. Perhaps she didn't. Maybe with no one else to turn to, she'd given up entirely.

Love's Pursuit

But notice, when everyone else rejected her, God showed up. Not only did He show up, but He sought her out (v. 7).

This is where the story gets intriguing. Scholars believe Hagar was speaking to someone much more powerful than an archangel or divine messenger, and here's why: In verse 9, who does this Angel say will give Hagar descendants?

According to verse 13, who spoke to her that day in the wilderness?

Could it be that she encountered not one of God's representatives that day but Christ, the Savior of the world? That, in that bleak and forsaken place, she personally experienced El Roi, the God who sees?

Notice, in that moment, her emphasis wasn't on what she'd experienced or what He had promised, but on God Himself. A God who became deeply personal. The God who sees.

How might this divine revelation have changed her perspective and soothed her pain?

How might her encounter have strengthened her to return to her home and all the dysfunction surrounding it?

When have you most needed to feel seen?

Whatever you're going through, even if you feel rejected and alone, know this: your Creator, your Savior, sees you. He's with you. He's seeking you out and drawing you near, in love. Nothing—not the actions of others or even your own—can irrevocably distance you from God's grace.

He is the God who sees.

Day Five
God's Power in Our Insufficiencies
Review: Genesis 16:4-15
Read: Judges 6:11-16; 7:1-7

God's mercy, sovereignty, and love provide the lens that allows us to reinterpret our past, present, and ultimately, ourselves. As we've seen, our greatest failures and moments of deepest pain can reveal the depth of God's love and grace. Because here's the story of grace: we are fatally flawed and critically insufficient. But Christ makes up for everything we lack, and in Him, we are enough.

We see this theme revealed, again and again, as we follow Sarah's journey from barrenness, and the feelings of worthlessness that likely accompanied this, to motherhood and being a recipient of grace. We saw with Hagar as well when, at her lowest state, when all seemed hopeless and perhaps she'd even given up the will to carry on, she encountered the God who sees.

Freed in Love

Sarah's story, ultimately, is about a God who looks down on His beloved daughters and says, "You have value—apart from what you do or don't do. In Me, you are enough."

This realization frees us from shame, regret, and fear of failure and allows us to come fully alive.

Let me give an example. I have numerous issues that hinder my ability to lead. I can be impatient and have emotional triggers that, unchecked, can lead to reactive rather than proactive behavior. As a creative visionary, I can confuse my team members with an abundance of ideas and leave those who are detail-oriented frustrated.

Knowing all this, when I sensed God nudging me into my current leadership role, I resisted. I was excited about the prospect of helping women find greater emotional and spiritual freedom; I just felt someone else would be much better suited for the job. I was terrified, should God expand my reach and influence, I'd do or say something to completely mess things up.

Although honestly, I was really afraid of looking bad—of experiencing rejection. So long as I could be selective with my interactions, so long as I never put myself in a position where my sponge of dirty water became squeezed, everything would be fine, I'd maintain my friends, and others wouldn't know how sinful and flawed I really was.

Dependence

My fear stemmed from a misplaced identity and insufficient understanding of grace. God rectified this by directing me to Exodus 3, when He commissioned Moses, an equally reluctant leader, to liberate His people from slavery. "Who am I to do this," Moses asked, to which God responded, "I Am"—the ever-present, all sufficient One. (Exodus 3). All Moses could see were his insufficiencies, but God wasn't relying on Moses. On the contrary. Moses needed to learn to rely fully on God, who was more than sufficient, and find success in Him.

This was so easy to see in Moses' life but so hard to apply to my own! At least, so long as I obsessed about myself. When I shifted my focus, however, onto God and His redemptive mission, my insecurities and fears lost their power. This is true for all of us. Focusing on who God is, on His grace and power in us, frees us to live authentically and fully engaged. This grace-based freedom allows us to become the women Christ created us to be.

Can you see the irony here? By hiding those parts of us we wish we weren't, we become less than what God designed, a fractured and dulled version of ourselves, if you will.

Grace-Based Growth

Standing on the other side of my decision to say yes, when God asked me to lead "Wholly Loved Ministries," I'm in awe over all the growth He's initiated through my surrender. I've learned lessons I otherwise never would have and discovered strengths and passions I might've overlooked.

That's not to say my obedience didn't involve pain and moments of failure. Far from it. In fact, nearly everything I feared might happen did. At times, I responded in ways I wish I hadn't, reacted out of past hurts rather than reality, and watched all of my weaknesses wreak havoc in some way. But through all the gunk, something radiated brighter—God's grace. With every mistake, I became a little less self-reliant, a little more surrendered, and a lot freer.

I learned to accept my failings without letting them paralyze me.

One day, completely flustered with me and my imperfections, a team member let me have it. For about ten minutes, she listed all my many faults. A year prior, I probably would've become defensive and made excuses or lashed out in kind. But having sunk deeper into grace, I was able to smile and say, "You're right. And here's how I'm going to work on those things."

Living in Grace

I recognized failure only revealed what I already knew to be true—I needed Jesus! I needed His grace, and praise God, I had it! That meant I didn't need to be perfect and had no reason to feel ashamed. I simply needed to lean further into Him and let Him continue to grow me.

But here's the real beauty of that whole scenario. I've learned the hardest and ugliest parts of my story have led to the most amazing spiritual conversations. In seeing God's mercy revealed in me—in us—others come to understand it's available to them also.

When I honestly evaluate my story in light of grace, a common thread emerges: Relying on my wisdom, strength, or abilities inevitably leads to failure and regret. Surrendering to Jesus, however, changes everything.

Pursued Despite Weakness

Consider Gideon's battle experience, revealed in Judges 6-7. Scripture tells us the Midianites had raided the Israelites' land and oppressed them to the point of starvation. So they cried out to God for help, which God provided, through a man who deemed himself woefully inadequate.

Where does Judges 6:11 say Gideon was when the Angel of the Lord approached him?

Why was he threshing wheat in that location? What does this show about his state of mind?

How does the Angel of the Lord refer to Gideon in verse 12?

Based on Gideon's reply, does he view himself in this way?

Underline "Go in the strength you have" (or however your translation states this) in your Bible. Does anything about this phrase resonate with you, and if so, how?

Why was it important Gideon remembered God was the One sending him on this mission (Judges 6:14b)?

Based on Gideon's response in verse 15, how does he view himself?

When have you viewed yourself in a similar fashion?

How does God respond in verse 16 to Gideon's statement?

How might recognizing and meditating on God's presence help you when you feel inadequate, insecure, or afraid?

In the account that follows, Gideon summoned up an army 32,000 strong (Judges 6:34-35, 7:1-3), which God promptly whittled down to 300. 300 beaten-down, oppressed Israelites ready to fight against a powerful people group so numerous, they were "like swarms of locusts" that were "impossible to count" (Judges 6:5, NLT).

Where Strength is Found

In other words, Gideon and his men were outmanned and outmuscled—by God's design.

According to Judges 7:2, why did God thin Gideon's men down to 300?

Pause to think about a time when you were forced to rely on God's strength. When was this, and what did the situation teach you about Him? What did it teach you about yourself? What did it teach you about grace?

Close today's study time in prayer, asking God to help you rely on and rest in His strength made perfect in your weakness as you go about your daily tasks. Ask Him to remind you that you don't have to "be enough" because He is enough for you and all you'll encounter or experience.

Week Seven: Living in Grace

Jennifer Slattery

Order of completion:

<u>Large Group time:</u>

- Discuss last week's lessons on pages 103-117 and share anything that resonated with you or surprised you in the reading.

- Watch Becoming His Princess Week Six: Moving Past Self-Sufficiency Video found on the Wholly Loved Ministries' YouTube channel (Search YouTube + Wholly Loved).

- Discuss the video as a group using the discussion questions on page 121.

<u>Home lessons:</u>

- Day one: Choose one of the 2 options provided on pages 123 and 125.
- Complete the remaining week's lessons as provided.

Week Seven
Viewer & Group Discussion Guide
From the Video:

Consider: Do you offer others the same grace you wish they'd offer you?

Our actions each day show the _____ and _____ of grace.

In Christ, we have _____ upon _____, enough to cover our biggest failings and worst mistakes.

We can't draw strength from a _____ power source.

In Christ, we find life _____ and come alive in the _____ and _____.

Through Jesus, God does what we can't— _____ us to Himself, and He _____ _____ _____ what we'll never become on our own—children of the promise.

The Promised Land points to _____, and the child of promise points to _____.

To grab hold of the life that Jesus offers, we first need to recognize how truly _____ we are apart from Him.

His love doesn't _____ when we return it or _____ when we push Him away.

But to truly _____ Christ's love and grace, we must choose to live under it.

He's the only _____ we can stand on, our only hope for _____, and the only sure route to _____.

The grace that brought us salvation is _____ and _____ and _____ enough to carry to completion the amazing and life-changing work God began in us.

No matter what you've done or where you've been, here's God's promise to you: "If you confess with your mouth that Jesus is Lord and believe in your heart that God raised Him from the dead, you will be saved" (Romans 12:9, ESV).

Group Discussion Questions:

Note to leaders: You probably won't have time to get to all the questions. Please let the discussion guide you, and focus on those questions you feel most beneficial to your group members.

What resonated with you most during last week's lessons or Bible reading?

What resonated with you most during the video?

Generally speaking, do you think people tend to give themselves or others more grace? Can you give some examples?

What are some ways we "make allowances" for our faults, either in our minds or in defense of our actions when confronted?

Can you share a time when someone showed you grace (didn't treat you as your sin or mistake deserved)? What was your emotional or behavioral response?

How does showing others grace reveal the gospel or Jesus?

How does showing ourselves grace reveal the gospel or Jesus?

What does it mean to live connected to Jesus?

How does staying connected to Jesus empower us to live as He desires?

Can you think of a time when you felt weak, angry, frightened, or uncertain and found power and strength through Bible reading or prayer?

What are some ways you can live more closely connected to Jesus during the week ahead?

How does knowing that God's love for you won't increase or decrease help you live in His grace?

Day One (Option One)
Understanding God's Big Picture Story
Read: Genesis 17

Who are the main characters in this passage?

What does this passage reveal about the human condition, such as:
- Mankind's rebellion against/obedience toward God?

- Mankind's attempts to fill their needs apart from Him or relying on Him for their needs?

- Mankind's attempts to reach Him on their own terms?

What does this passage reveal regarding God's nature?

What does this passage reveal about God's plans?

How might this passage reveal mankind's need for the gospel?

In what ways are you/have you been similar to one or more of the characters in this passage?

What might God want you to know through this section of Scripture?

What might He be asking you to do?

End your reading in prayer, asking God to help you apply His word and live out whatever you sense Him impressing on your heart.

Day One (Option Two)
Bible Study Application Tool: Cross References
Read: Genesis 17; Romans 3:10-11, 4:1-3, 16-17; Galatians 3:7-9, 15-16, 4:23

My daughter hates watching television anywhere near me because she knows she'll be confronted with countless questions. Most of these arise from my tendency to pop in when something intrigues me and out when I become bored. As a result, one could liken my understanding to Swiss cheese—solid in parts but permeated with holes.

Do you ever feel a similar confusion when reading Scripture? How about when a passage in the New Testament points to something that occurred thousands of years previously? And what about those books like Daniel or Isaiah that are said to have dual meanings that reveal events occurring during the prophet's lifetime and after Jesus' birth?

This is when the beauty and mystery of Scripture is most revealed, because only a Creator outside time and space, with power over both, could weave together such a coherent, interconnected book. One that utilizes all the literary tools such as foreshadowing, themes, characterization, climax, and culmination. But most importantly, it's a book that has changed countless lives.

Interconnected Truths

As we've already seen, every narrative in some way points to Jesus. Genesis 17 & 21 present perhaps the most compelling announcement of all. Our understanding of and appreciation for the truth and symbolism revealed through this child long promised to Sarah and Abraham deepens when we take time to read Scriptural cross references, such as those found in the book of Romans.

Many Bibles list cross references in the footnotes or margins. If you have your Bible handy, open it now to Genesis 17. In the first verse alone, you'll likely find six cross-referenced verses listed. Four of these come from the narrative we've been studying, one comes from Deuteronomy, and one from Matthew.

Let's look at a few examples:

Genesis 17:1, Matthew 5:48, and Deuteronomy 18:13.

What do these verses say to do?

What's our standard?

Was Abraham able to follow God's instructions in Genesis 17:1?

Has anyone been able to follow God faithfully and blamelessly?

How do these verses point to Jesus?

Now read Romans 4:1-3. How was Abraham made righteous?

Read Romans 4:16-17. According to these verses, how did Abraham become the father of many nations?

(If you have time, you may want to read all of Romans 4.)

Read Galatians 3:7-9. Who are Abraham's children?

According to Galatians 3:15-16, what is the significance of the word "seed"?

What does Galatians 4:23 say Hagar's and Sarah's sons illustrate?

According to Romans 3:10-11, why is it very good news that our righteousness comes through faith and not through "good works"?

End your time today prayerfully considering your life and relationship with God based on what you've read. Are you relying on good works or your faith in Jesus to make you right with God? And if the latter, are you resting consistently in that truth? What might need to change in order for you to do so? Ask God to help you apply His word and live out whatever you sense Him impressing on your heart.

Day Two
Investigating Historical Context
Review: Genesis 17

When we found out we were pregnant with our daughter, my husband and I spent hours reciting various names, sifting them through how they sounded, the image they evoked, and what nicknames—especially those created by their peers—they might initiate.

I'm sure many parents went through similar experiences. Names matter in every culture and time period. This was especially true in Bible times when a name was thought to describe a person's character or experience. It could record a significant birth experience, like when a hairy child was named Esau, which sounds like a Hebrew term meaning hair. This child's heel-grasping brother was named Jacob, which sounds like the Hebrew words for heel and deceiver (Gen. 25).

Follow Jacob to adulthood and we see he did indeed live up to his name when he swindled first his brother's birthright, and then his blessing. Decades later, however, he encountered God in a powerful and personal way, and then God changed his name.

Names in the Ancient World

If you're able, spend an evening researching the importance of names in ancient Mesopotamia and Palestine.

In today's passage, God changed Abraham's and Sarah's names as well. According to Genesis 17:3-6 and 15-16, why did He do this this?

How might understanding the significance of names, in historical context and also in Scripture, deepen your appreciation of what God did in this passage?

Considering their culture, how might Abraham and Sarah have felt to have their Creator directly change their names?

After this, would they be more apt to refer to themselves using the names others had given them or those ascribed directly by God? Why?

A Name to Live By

Which do you place more emphasis on? Though we discussed the topic of false versus grace-given names during our first week together, it bears a second mention here as we look at what it means to truly rest in grace.

What other customs mentioned in today's passage could you research further? Jot a short list now. If you have time, read an article or two on one of these topics.

Close your study time in prayer, reflecting on God's gift of grace and our need for it. Ask Him to help you live in the reality of His grace.

Day Three
Finding God When We Reach The End of Ourselves
Read: Genesis 18:1-15

In order to come to God—to live and rest in Him—we first need to become aware of our need. We humans are a prideful, self-deceived bunch. We like to think that we're self-sufficient. We set goals, make plans, work hard, and create our own destinies.

Or so we think, until our most diligent and carefully orchestrated plans fail. At that point, many of us quickly find and pursue Plan B, until that fails. Then we implement Plan C, then Plan D.

But woe to the woman who continually finds success! When all goes well and we have a series of achievements beneath us, we may begin to feel as if we don't need God. As we chase worldly gifts, victories, and blessings, we risk missing out on the greatest gift of all—God Himself.

Perhaps this is why, at times, God allows us to experience longing—so He can use our earthly heart cries to point us to something bigger.

Author Jessica Brodie's Story (Jessicabrodie.com):

I wanted a baby more than anything. And because I thought I was ready, I assumed it would be so.

God had other plans.

Instead, I found myself struggling with infertility. I tried all I was "supposed" to do—fertility treatments, stress-relief—but nothing worked. Frustration and despair forced me to my knees. Was I not "mother material"? Did God want me to adopt?

Finally, I saw myself in the Bible in Hannah's infertility journey (1 Samuel 1-2). I knew it then, that was why God hadn't let me get pregnant. There was nothing I could do. It was all up to God, and God wanted to make sure my child belonged to Him.

I squeezed my eyes shut, and an amazing peace settled over me. I vowed that if God allowed me to get pregnant, then I would commit my child to Him. Just like Hannah, I would make sure my child knew Him and was raised in faith.

That night, I slept in a blanket of contentment. It no longer mattered whether I got pregnant. What mattered was that as a mother, however or if ever it occurred, I would raise my child for the Lord. God was in control.

I did get pregnant, and that baby is now almost thirteen. Yet I have never let myself forget the promise I made God all those years ago.

While I didn't know it then, that promise was as much about me becoming a child of God as about me birthing a child dedicated to Him. My decision was a turning point: the precise moment I decided God was paramount.

I know God doesn't answer our prayers by giving us what we want or think we need. He gives us what He knows we need. I see now what I needed wasn't a child but a path to understanding that God, and total surrender to His will, was supreme. My infertility became my path to holy understanding.

In Genesis, Sarah wanted a son so God's promise to her husband, Abraham—that he'd be the father of nations—would come true. Yet she could not conceive. Instead of having faith that God would provide, she took matters into her own hands and turned to a surrogate, Hagar (Genesis 16).

But God had something different in mind—a miracle birth to a woman so far past the age of conception only God could have done something so great! This wonder-child, Isaac, became the father of countless generations, fulfilling God's promise and bringing about Sarah's healing.

God works His will through us and, sometimes, in spite of us. But make no mistake: He's in charge, not us.

(Find out more about Jessica by reading her bio at the end of the book.)

***

How long would you wait, in faith, for God to fulfill a promise to you? While you waited, would your faith waver? If years and then decades passed, and both you and your husband had sinned, would you worry God had rescinded? Would you worry your failings had perhaps nullified the terms of God's covenant?

Genesis 17:17 tells us Abraham was 100 years old when God revealed the final details of His promise. He made it clear Abraham and Sarah would indeed have a child, and not through their servants. This child would come from their holy union, revealing the sanctity of marriage, which in turn reveals the binding power of the gospel.

Can you see all the layers God wove through Abraham and Sarah's journey—all the "grace-sightings" He provided?

They'd been waiting, praying, and longing for a child for decades! But finally, the moment came. And after one unexpected encounter, Abraham and Sarah's lives were changed forever.

When the Waiting Nears Its End

According to Genesis 18:1, what was Abraham doing when the three visitors arrived? How did Abraham respond?

When has God shown up in the middle of your ordinary and turned your day into something extraordinary?

Abraham was alert and ready to act. Though he didn't know who these men were, he responded quickly, with integrity and hospitality. Can you share a time when you responded to a situation or person in a godly way and found yourself on God's path to blessing?

Read verses 9-12. Why do you think Sarah laughed?

At this point, do you believe Sarah and Abraham had any idea who these men were?

Do you think that impacted Sarah's reaction?

According to verse 13, who was Abraham speaking with?

Encounter With the Divine

Whenever you see LORD in all caps, you know *Yahweh*, God's formal yet personal name revealed in Exodus 3:15, was used.

In other words, Abraham was speaking to the great I Am, Yahweh. Not the God who once was or who may be, but who is and always will be.

Always present.
Always loving.
Always faithful.
Always righteous and true.
Always bestowing grace upon grace.

This is the God who met with Abraham face to face and reiterated His promise.

When God Acts

God alone would grant Abraham's and Sarah's desire, would meet their need, and would do what they couldn't do themselves.

God comes to us in our time of need as well. He showed this most beautifully when He took our sins upon Himself and died in our place, to rescue us from death and eternal damnation. Through Christ, He also meets us face to face—personally and intimately.

All He asks is that we open our hearts to Him. That we believe He is who He says He is, that He did what He said He did, and that He'll do what He promises to do.

In Abraham and Sarah, God demonstrated, in Christ, every promise is as good as done.

When has God felt most real to you?

How do you experience Yahweh, the God who *is*, in your day-to-day?

Close your time in prayer, asking God to help you become more alert to His presence and His love.

Day Four
Grace Enough For Every Failure
Read: Genesis 20:1-17

Do you ever feel like you keep making the same mistakes and landing in the same messes over and over? I do. And sometimes it seems the harder I try, the more I mess up.

Then again, that's most often my biggest problem—I try to live this Christian life in my own strength instead of resting in Christ. Relying on myself almost always leads to failure, followed by regret, and teeth-gritting determination to do better the next time, and the time after that, and the time after that.

It can be a joy-deflating, life-stealing cycle! I know I need to stay more consistently connected to Christ, but when I don't and my sinful tendencies take hold, I need to ground myself in what I know is true: God loves me and purchased me, sins and all, by His precious blood. He gave His all, His last dying breath, to free me from condemnation that I might live in grace.

Learning to Yield

Like every faithful parent, He longs for me to live up to my full potential in Him, to I daily yield to His Spirit within me. But He also knows I'm going to blow it. A lot. My bouts of rebellion, pride, and entitlement don't surprise Him. Nor do they negate His grace.

Rather, they make it all the more apparent.

When my nephew was in the "terrible twos," my sister told me a story. I don't remember his behaviors—plural—but they'd tested her last thread of patience on a daily—hourly—basis. (You may understand completely!)

But then one day, he obeyed—with a smile! There'd been no cajoling, bribing, or bartering. No fits, screams, or bared teeth. Watching him, joy filled my sister's heart. She thought, "This time, he got it right!"

I sometimes wonder if that's how God views us. He knows we'll throw a tantrum or two—give in to our pride and selfishness. Maybe even make a ginormous mess of things. But every once in a while, through prayer and surrender and utter trust in Him, we get it right. We live in and then live out His grace—reveal His love and mercy to others, form bridges instead of barriers, and demonstrate, with depth and clarity, Christ in us. When that happens, He celebrates. Likely, another tantrum will come, but in that moment, we got it right.

In other words, He recognizes we're often still in those terrible twos, but He knows maturity is coming.

That maturity comes when we spend more time with Him and surrender to the stirrings of the Holy Spirit. That is the only way we can truly live out our faith.

Mankind's Faithlessness

Recognizing my own faithless, fearful, and sinful tendencies helps me understand, in part, some of Abraham's behaviors.

I say in part because had I been Sarah, I would've ...

Actually, I'm not sure what I would've done. She really didn't have many choices. It wasn't like she could leave Abraham. Where would she go? She couldn't get a job or stay at a woman's shelter, though she'd have ample reason to.

Shelter director: *Were you abused?*
Sarah: *Does being pimped out to other men count?*

Seriously, by this point in our narrative, Abraham had betrayed Sarah twice! And these weren't minor betrayals. His selfishness and lies left Sarah completely defenseless—according to human perspective. But as we saw in both cases, when her husband betrayed and abandoned her, her Father God showed up and took care of business.

Imagine the statement God's rescue made to her rejected heart!

God's Faithfulness

Here's a truth we can rely on: Mankind's failure never negates grace—not the sins we commit, nor the sins others commit against us. Maybe that's why Scripture is filled with stories of sinful men and women who are not only rescued by God, but are actually used by Him.

One afternoon, while studying Romans, I asked my professor how Abraham, who'd clearly shown evidence of fear—of not believing God—could be listed as an example of faith. In chapter 12, Abraham's behavior was a little more understandable. After all, God hadn't been all that clear regarding the details of the promise. Abraham may have assumed his descendants would come through another wife, as was the custom. This happened with Jacob, a man who came later and birthed the twelve tribes of Israel. Or maybe he thought, should he die, one of his servants would carry on his name and occupy his land, similar to how a kinsman redeemer might.

But today's passage directly follows Abraham's encounter with God in chapter 17. Had he forgotten about the vision? The name change? That God had clearly and directly revealed that the long promised child would come from his own seed and Sarah's womb?

How could he doubt what God had disclosed in such a supernatural way? I wanted to understand why Abraham, after his examples of faithlessness, was listed among the heroes of faith in Hebrews 11.

My professor's response: How can we, who act faithlessly multiple times a day, be considered people of faith?

In other words, grace isn't dependent on our ability to respond perfectly, but on our reliance on the only One who can and always does.

This is one of the most powerful messages woven throughout Scripture. It's also very plainly displayed in today's and tomorrow's passages.

According to verse two, how did Abraham introduce Sarah?

What was the result?

How did God respond (v. 3)?

I'm tempted to want to place the blame entirely on Abraham, but according to verse 5, what role did Sarah play in their deception?

I don't know if she felt she had no other choice, or if she genuinely agreed with her husband's plans. Regardless, they both lied, and as a result, an entire nation nearly suffered the consequences.

The Importance of Integrity

Lying always hurts others, but it damages our credibility most of all. How can our honesty (or lack thereof) impact how others receive our claims regarding God and the gospel?

How did God respond to Abraham's betrayal (v. 6-7)?

What justification does Abraham give in verses 11-13?

What are some ways we attempt to justify our sin?

When did Abraham first decide to lie about Sarah (v. 13)?

What does that indicate regarding his emotions upon leaving?

The NIV says Abraham states it this way: "And when God had me wander from my father's household, I said to her, 'This is how you can show your love for me: Everywhere we go, say of me, "He is my brother."'"

How does that statement reveal a false notion of love?

In what ways is God's love different from the kind of love we might be used to or encounter?

How is Jesus the greatest expression of God's love?

As you close today's study, take a moment to thank God for His unyielding and unconquerable grace and ask Him to help you learn to live more consistently in it.

Day Five
No Greater Love
Read: Genesis 22

Can you imagine waiting and praying for something, for decades, only to have it snatched from your hands? Or harder still, to sense God asking you to let that thing go? I've experienced numerous "surrender" moments throughout my writing career—when my hold on the gift began to overshadow my heart for the Giver.

When my dream became my god.

Jesus knows all those little, insufficient gods you and I cling to will never fill us the way He can. So, being the faithful, loving, freedom-giving Savior that He is, He beckons us to let go.

To release our grip on all those things clogging our hearts in order to give Him the preeminence He deserves.

That's not so easy, is it? To surrender completely, entrusting ourselves and everything we love to God?

Of everything I've surrendered, my daughter has been the most difficult, frightening, and at times, painful. Honestly, this is something I fight daily—to entrust her, willingly and completely, to the One who loves her deeply.

I seem to do so in bits and pieces, committing her to Jesus in one moment then attempting to grab her back the next!

Surrendering His Treasure

I cannot imagine the pain Abraham must have felt the morning he saddled his donkey and took his beloved son and two of his servants and set out to sacrifice Isaac. I wish we could see his interaction with Sarah beforehand! Did she know what his plans were? Or did she think he was merely going to offer a sacrifice, like he had so many times before?

How would you respond if God had asked of you what he did of Abraham?

Would you barter with Him? Beg Him to change His command? Ignore His voice entirely? Maybe even run the other way?

How does God describe Abraham's son in verse two?

What does this indicate to you?

God knew precisely how difficult and painful this task would be for Abraham. He'd heard his and Sarah's prayers for a child over the decades. He'd witnessed Sarah's joyful laughter once she finally conceived. He was present when they'd celebrated his birth and at every special moment since.

But still He asked. Why?

God's Higher Plans

Could it be God planned to use their pain for something bigger, something deeper and more eternal?

Could it be He was making His Son's life more personal—showing us precisely how much Christ's death cost Father and Son? And yet, both paid the price willingly, for you and me.

When you read this chapter, who do you most empathize with?

What does this reveal about God's heart—for Jesus and for us?

Jesus paid an incredible price to free us from our sins and all of our striving. He created us, in love, to have an intimate relationship with us. But Scripture says each one of us have spurned His love and rebelled against Him. We've sinned, and our sin distances us from our holy God. Worse, our sin enslaves us.

But when Jesus died, He took our sin and the punishment we deserve upon Himself. With His death and resurrection, He conquered death and the power of sin once and for all. And He offered us a precious gift—eternal life, spent connected to Him. To receive this life, all we must do is believe He is who He says He is and did what He said He did.

Have you received His gift of life? If not, you can today. Simply turn to Him in prayer, admit that you've lived contrary to His truth and His will, that you believe He's God's sinless Son who died in your place, and ask Him to take control of your life. If you pray this, and you truly mean it, you can know you are now forever held secure, in grace by grace.

Read and compare John 19:17 with Genesis 22:6. How are these verses similar?

Scholars aren't sure what Abraham meant in verse 8 when he assured Isaac that God would provide the sacrificial lamb. But regardless of his understanding at that particular moment, God made the truth of Abraham's statement clear in verse 13.

Grace Revealed

This is where the beauty of this event—and really of Sarah and Abraham's entire life—is revealed. Their story, including the most painful moments, point to Jesus, the only One able to bring light into our darkness, hope from our despair, and life to those things once considered dead.

This is where our study ends as well. Remember where we started—with that barren, seemingly cursed woman from the ancient city of Ur? The one who was overlooked, devalued, rejected, abandoned, and betrayed?

She's far from that woman by the time her story ends. Instead, she's seen, chosen, rescued and redeemed, elevated and honored not because of anything she did but rather what God did in and through her.

She became God's princess, and I have no doubt she sits as His princess today, basking in His love and grace.

May we do the same.

Visit Wholly Loved Ministries online at whollyloved.com for more resources that will help you grow in your faith.

Get to Know the Authors:

Susan Aken is a homemaker, substitute teacher, and writer. She lives in Nebraska but was born and raised in Oklahoma. Her greatest love is for the Lord Jesus Christ who has redeemed her and set her free. Her other loves are her husband, son, and daughter-in-law to be. Susan enjoys reading, photography, spending time with family and friends, writing, and sitting down with a cup of tea. She has a heart for prayer ministry and loves her church! Visit her online at susanaken53.wordpress.com

Jessica Brodie is a Christian author, award-winning journalist, editor, blogger, and writing coach. She is the editor of the *South Carolina United Methodist Advocate*, the oldest continuously published newspaper in Methodism. For her newspaper, she has authored a devotional, More Like Jesus: A Devotional Journey, plus edited an anthology of racial narratives, *Stories of Racial Awakening: Narratives of Changed Hearts and Lives*. She is a member of Mount Horeb United Methodist Church in Lexington, South Carolina, with her husband, Matt, and their four preteen children. Learn more about her fiction and read her faith blog, Shining the Light, at http://jessicabrodie.com.

Cheri Cowell is an author, speaker, and sidewalk theologian. She's the author of four books, including the award-winning, *365 Devotions For Peace*, which sold in Cracker Barrel. She is the author of two Bible studies, *One Story, One Mission, One God*, and *Parables and Word Pictures*, and two books on spiritual growth, *Direction: Discernment for the Decisions of Your Life* and *Living the Story*. Cheri has a degree from Asbury Theological Seminary and she loves to share how God's Word applies to the sidewalk issues of life because, as Cheri shares, "life is not always easy but God has answers." Cheri has been married to her wonderful husband, Randy, for over 33 years and they call Orlando Florida home for most of the year. When they aren't there or visiting National Parks they're enjoying their cabin–a piece of paradise–in the Smokey Mountains of Tennessee.

Dena Dyer is the author or co-author of ten books, including the award-winning *Wounded Women of the Bible: Finding Hope when Life Hurts* with Tina Samples (Kregel). Her most fun book to pen was written with her husband Carey: *Love at First Fight: 52 Story-Based Meditations for Married Couples* (Barbour). Over the past two decades, she has had hundreds of articles published on blogs, websites, and in magazines and newspapers. Her credits include *Reader' Digest, Writer's Digest, Family Circle, Parenting,* and *Redbook*.

In Dena's day job, she serves as Director of Communications and Development at a crisis pregnancy center. She and Carey (who is a worship pastor) have been married twenty-one wonderful years and a couple more they don't talk about. They live in Texas with their two sons (Jordan and Jackson) and a spoiled dog, Princess. Dena loves to read, cook, watch British "telly," scour thrift stores for great finds, and spend time with family and friends.

Jennifer Slattery is a multi-published author and speaker who's addressed women's groups, church groups, Bible studies, and other writers across the nation. She's the author of numerous contemporary novels, including the reader-acclaimed *Breaking Free* and her latest release *Restoring*

Her Faith. She blogs for Crosswalk (owned by Salem Communications), and maintains a devotional blog found at *http://jenniferslatterylivesoutloud.com*. She has a passion for helping women discover, embrace, and live out who they are in Christ. As the founder of Wholly Loved Ministries, (*Whollyloved.com*) she and her team partner with churches to facilitate events designed to help women rest in their true worth and live with maximum impact. When not writing, reading, or editing, Jennifer loves going on mall dates with her adult daughter and coffee dates with her hilariously fun husband.

Get to Know The Editors:

Yvonne Anderson is a proud wife, mom and grandma, who has been following Jesus for more than forty years now and growing in her love for Him each day. She has written several Christian sci-fi novels and has also been employed as a legal assistant, virtual assistant and church secretary. While subsequent years have honed her writing skills, Yvonne prefers editing to drafting. She especially enjoys helping other writers discover their voice and sharpen their focus on the gospel that saves. She blogs occasionally at YsWords.com.

LaShawn Montoya holds a B.A. in English Literature from the University of CA, Davis, and as you'd expect with a degree like that, reads voraciously and loves to help edit all types of copy, from advertisements to novels and everything in between. She has over 20 years of vocational ministry experience and her husband is currently on staff at a large church in Nebraska. LaShawn especially enjoys working with school- aged children (and has 3 grown children of her own and cannot wait to become a grandmother someday!).

Made in the USA
Columbia, SC
16 February 2019